First Freedom First

MIKE KEEFE, DENVER POST

FIRST FREEDOM FIRST

A Citizens' Guide to
Protecting Religious Liberty
and the Separation
of Church and State

Reverend Dr. C. Welton Gaddy
Reverend Barry W. Lynn

Beacon Press, Boston

BEACON PRESS

25 Beacon Street

Boston, Massachusetts 02108-2892

www.beacon.org

Beacon Press books
are published under the auspices of
the Unitarian Universalist Association of Congregations.

11 10 09 08   8 7 6 5 4 3 2 1

This book is printed on acid-free paper that meets the uncoated paper
ANSI/NISO specifications for permanence as revised in 1992.

Composition by Wilsted and Taylor Publishing Services

Library of Congress Cataloging-in-Publication Data

Gaddy, C. Welton.
  First freedom first : a citizens' guide to protecting religious liberty
and the separation of church and state / C. Welton Gaddy, Barry W. Lynn.
     p. cm.
  ISBN 978-0-8070-4224-3 (alk. paper)
 1. Freedom of religion—United States. I. Lynn, Barry W. II. Title.

 BR516.G33 2008
 323.44'20973—dc22   2007038367

Contents

RESOURCES: A CALL TO ACTION

Preface: A Personal Perspective: The Freedom That Makes America America

ANDREW S. GROVE

It was as if there was an invisible border in the middle of the Atlantic Ocean. We crossed it at the moment some of my fellow refugees came back from a Sunday service.

It was January of 1957 and I was on a ship, a World War II troop
carrier rescued from mothball storage and given a reprieve, that
was carrying 1,600 Hungarian refugees from a port in Germany to
the United States. I was one of them. I was twenty years old, cold,
shabby, scared, and excited. I had left my family and my old life
behind, committing the rest of my life to a new country I knew
nothing about. A group of young refugees approached me looking
indignant, even angry. "It's ridiculous," they sputtered. I quickly
learned that what was ridiculous was the sermon they just heard
from a Hungarian American minister who had come along to give
spiritual guidance to the new immigrants. He had focused his sermon on the emphatic suggestion that every member of his tran-
sient congregation must leave antisemitism behind.

As a Jew, I found it very upsetting to listen to my fellow refugees
bemoan the prospect of living without antisemitism. And it was
not surprising that they made these comments to me—knowing
full well that I was a Jew. Life in Hungary had always been characterized by antisemitism. I learned this at age five, when a little girl
I played with in the park told me that Jews like me would be pushed

into the Danube River because we killed Jesus Christ. By the time I was nine, this had become reality.

Antisemitism had been an integral part of the fabric of Hungarian society long before I was born. In her youth my mother had been an aspiring concert pianist but was refused admission to the State Academy of Music. The rejection was delivered with an off-hand comment that "this is not a place for Jewish girls."

What happened to 500,000 Hungarian Jews is well known. Their fate constituted some of the bloodier chapters of Adolph Eichmann's Final Solution. Less well known is how common and hurtful antisemitism was among ordinary Hungarians. During the Nazi occupation, some of our neighbors reported one of their own for bringing us food after we were evicted from our apartment house. They exposed him, knowing that his act of kindness was potentially punishable by death, both his and ours. The neighbors in question were people with whom we had lived in peace in the same apartment house for decades, who had always said friendly hellos when we passed on the staircase.

How could they act this way? What made them do it? Economic benefit may have been what caused them to pick our apartment clean of our belongings while we were gone. I could understand that, even though I could not forgive it. But hostile—even lethal—action taken toward people with whom they had never had an unpleasant encounter, for no evident gain, was hard for me to understand. Decades after Eichmann was executed, my resentment about being the object of such antisemitism remains unabated.

We lived in the same house, we shopped at the same stores, and we hid together in the cellar when English and American airplanes dropped bombs on us, yet there was a lethal divide. What separated us? It was religion. They were Christians, Catholics, Lutherans. We were Jews. Not religious Jews, but that made no difference.

The government was an active participant. As the war progressed toward its final stages, increasingly vicious restrictions were imposed on Hungarians of Jewish descent, culminating in thousands being sent to the gas chamber or pushed into the icy Danube. Anybody who gave us aid was also threatened with execution.

There were posters detailing in frightening language the penalties that would ensue. Their images are still with me. I would have been paralyzed from helping anyone in the face of such threats.

When the Communists took over Hungary, religion was gradually banished. But the hatred and distrust between Jews and non-Jews remained; they just had to be hidden from sight. What happened on the deck of the troop carrier in the middle of the Atlantic Ocean was this suppressed antagonism bubbling over and becoming visible.

The Communists may have put a lid on traditional religion, but in their stead they brought a new state-supported "theology." Where before people justified turning against their neighbors on the authority of their God, the new theology provided cover for similar acts, with "the Party" becoming the one supreme authority, one that you could not challenge or argue with.

True believers were the scariest. When a well-known Communist official was suddenly deposed and tried for crimes that were improbable in the extreme, we all listened to the radio broadcast of his trial and heard how he had confessed to crimes that he never could have committed. Later, when the truth about his imprisonment became known, the most shocking finding was that he had gone along with the false charges for "the good of the Party." In the eyes of such true believers, the Party was never wrong, could never be wrong, even if its members were bloody criminals.

Prior to Communism, I had been told in religion classes—in no uncertain terms—not to argue with the teachings of religious doctrine, even when they were implausible and completely at odds with what I had learned in a history or science class the hour before. Communist dogma was taught with the same requirements of suspending logic and disregarding personal observation, history, or science. To argue, to analyze, to question were very dangerous. It was so for us students and for respected scholars. Later, I learned of biologists who were put to death for running experiments whose findings deviated from official Communist Party dogma on the role of genetics.

So, hearing about the minister's sermon on the ship had a very different effect on me than on my fellow refugees. It promised an America where I might be allowed to live without being told by God or Party what to think, what to believe, and how to act.

Fifty years have passed. I can say without hesitation that my expectations were fulfilled. To be sure, from time to time there were attempts to convert me. Some fellow students in college wanted me to adopt the tenets of the Jewish religion. Later, coworkers invited me to a discussion group ostensibly organized to study and analyze the teachings of the Bible in terms of what we know today of biblical times. This interested me, but I found that the real purpose of the group was to proselytize me. This encounter set off alarms in my head, reminding me of past events, and I never returned to the group.

These incidents were reminiscent of Hungary, but there was a huge difference: I could and did say no in both instances and I didn't feel the slightest coercion from my school or my employer, and especially not from the government.

Not that the government doesn't know how to apply pressure. I have had some hints of what the state—in this case the federal government—could do if it got obsessed. When I listened to the hearings of the House Committee on Un-American Activities, I shivered. Memories of the political trial of the interior minister in Hungary came back to me. The defendants in each case were charged with political actions that were the polar opposites of each other. But the trial ambiance, the traveling hearings, the repeated testimonies, the pressure on the witnesses, and the phrasing of those who buckled under this pressure were similar enough to scare me. These hearings disabused me of any notion that it could not happen here. It could and it did, yet opposing forces eventually curtailed the reach of this pressure. I gradually concluded that America is different. It is set apart from much of the world; in so many countries neighbors chase neighbors out of their home of many years (if they do not kill each other first) based on religious or political differences. In contrast, Americans are Americans, with nationality, political belief, and religion being points of distinction but not points of contention. This has made America America, and it has made me a ferociously proud citizen.

In the last few years, I have observed increasing attempts to weaken this characteristic. The language of politics contains more frequent religious references, and political positions are buttressed more and more by reliance on private communication between the politician and his/her God. The use of God's name in place of rational arguments is becoming more frequent. This trend frightens me. I have seen what people can do in the name of their God. I would prefer to base the questions of life on facts, systems of laws, and science.

The last, science, has been threatened in this same time period in a way that I could not imagine even ten years ago. Decades after the system of justice ruled in favor of teaching evolution in schools, the issue has resurfaced. This is stunning. We have witnessed incredible developments in the time between the Scopes trial and the contemporary version, the doctrine of Intelligent Design. Nuclear power, the human genome, the microchip, and the Internet have arrived. The life expectancy of the citizens of this country has increased by some twenty years. Supercomputers can predict weather patterns in detail and locate oil deep underground. All of these are achievements—designs—of human intelligence. How can we not celebrate the power of rationality?

Then, when highly placed officers of our armed forces use the phrases of religion to motivate the soldiers under their command, I feel even more strongly that we are at a dangerous juncture. The invisible border in the Atlantic where I discovered the America that was to be my home fifty years ago seems to be moving in the wrong direction.

I have profound respect for the human mind, its power to reason and to communicate. Yet beliefs have also been part of my life. They are personal in nature. They are mine and mine alone. On the rare occasion when I try to share them with others, I find language insufficient for the task. Music expresses my beliefs more eloquently. The soaring themes of *Panis Angelicus* can lift me up and Verdi's *Dies Irae* can give me determination and courage.

I have never written about my beliefs because they are, well, mine alone. They help me to understand and deal with the issues of my life. They may or may not work for another. Imposing one person's interpretation of beliefs on another is what I escaped from. Different beliefs have also been the cause of persecution of neighbors by neighbors in Hungary and in Bosnia, in the Middle East and in Africa.

Our Founding Fathers were believers who saw the need to keep neighbors from turning on neighbors because of their own personal beliefs. In an incredible act of foresight, they set down protections against this in language that still rings modern and true today. This is where our first freedom made its first appearance. Today's battle to reinvigorate that freedom is not the first and will not be the last. But it is as important today as it was then.

This freedom created America. Maintaining it maintains America.

"Congress shall make no law respecting an establishment of religion, or prohibiting the free exercise thereof; or abridging the freedom of speech, or of the press; or the right of the people peaceably to assemble, and to petition the government for a redress of grievances."

UNITED STATES CONSTITUTION,
Bill of Rights, Amendment I

"That congress shall make no law respecting; I mean it tells you that the church and the government, the religion and the government are two separate things and you have a choice and they shouldn't go around telling me what I need to do."

FIRST FREEDOM FIRST focus group member, Cleveland

Introduction

C. WELTON GADDY

Religious freedom is in big trouble in the United States. That means democracy is in trouble, religion is in trouble, and, given the foundational importance of religious freedom—our first freedom—for all other freedoms, our whole way of life is in trouble.

The crisis fed by diminishing interest in and support for religious freedom will worsen exponentially if it is not addressed responsibly, effectively, broadly, and quickly. Such is the disturbing context in which this book has been written. Such is the stark reality that serves as the backdrop against which this book should be read.

THE CRISIS RELATED TO RELIGIOUS FREEDOM

The United States is now the most religiously pluralistic nation in the world. For that reason alone, religious freedom is more important than ever. Currently, however, a majority of the American people, including many media pundits, church leaders, and government officials, are functioning with a false assumption—that the United States has an established religion, that America is a *Christian* nation. Subsequently, often no more than a condescending nod is given to any other religious tradition. Virtually no attention at all, much less public acknowledgment, is devoted to people who choose not to embrace any religion. The historic constitutional principles that have provided our nation with a formula for unity amid diversity, and cooperation despite division, are now the subject of criticism. Actually, some public spokespersons even blame these fundamental principles of democracy and their advocates for fomenting a runaway secularism and dangerous liberalism that are, according to these critics, ruining the nation.

A well-financed, self-appointed wrecking crew has set its sights on pummeling to the point of destruction Thomas Jefferson's metaphor of a wall of separation between church and state. Tactics of these tear-down-the-wall opponents of religious liberty include deliberate misrepresentations of the meaning of church-state separation. Wide-eyed extremists with exceptionally loud voices wrongly claim that Jefferson's historic metaphor of church-state separation forbids religion from having anything to do with politics and government. Stirring tremors of paranoia, these strident voices point to church-state separation as the culprit to blame for the absence of moral values in politics and government. Opponents of religious liberty label supporters of religious liberty as people hostile to religion, people who must be stopped and/or silenced for the nation to be preserved. Such critics take pride in their efforts to give "the separation of church and state" a bad name.

An uninformed public—eager for simplicity, desirous of being part of a majority, anxiously longing for security, and susceptible to anyone who comes along pointing to the one cause of the nation's problems and the one solution that will fix everything—is vulnerable to manipulation and misinformation. Many citizens have bought into the declarations of destruction heralded by people whose motivation is to alter the Constitution and construct an establishment of religion—*their* religion—in this nation. The architectural designs for this new configuration of government and religion have been drawn in high places, financed generously, and praised as rich resources for preserving "the faith." I am sad to write that the campaign against religious freedom is working.

PUBLIC OPINION AND RELIGIOUS FREEDOM

Observing and listening to the American public provides insight into the effectiveness of those who seek the demise of the religion clauses in the First Amendment to the Constitution. The Religious Right has been surprisingly successful in its strategy of misinforming and/or disillusioning people about the First Amendment to our Constitution and the history surrounding it. I find much of the relevant polling data disturbing.

- *The United States is now the most religiously diverse nation in the world. Yet Americans overwhelmingly consider the United States a Christian nation. At least 67 percent of the public characterizes the nation as Christian (Pew Research Center for the People and the Press, August 24, 2006).*

- *Though the United States Constitution forbids a public test for candidates seeking election to public office, 70 percent of the voters want the president of the United States to be "a person of faith" (Pew Research Center for the People and & the Press, September 20, 2000).*

- *Polling by the First Freedom Center in October 2005 documents "a conflicted citizenry" when it comes to understanding, much less supporting, religious liberty. Though 74 percent of the people think that religious liberty is as important as ever, 50 percent of those people think that the separation of church and state is not necessary (23 percent) or that church-state separation should be interpreted less strictly (27 percent). In an earlier poll, the First Freedom Center found that, besides freedom of speech, a majority of the respondents (52 percent) ranked religious freedom as the most important constitutional right, with 84 percent indicating that religious freedom was more important than when it was first established. However, a whopping 49 percent of the respondents thought that keeping religion and government separate was unnecessary or too strictly enforced (First Freedom Center, September 14, 2004).*

- *There is little wonder that rampant ambivalence characterizes public attitudes regarding this precious but fragile freedom. Many Americans cannot identify the document that guarantees religious freedom. In one poll, 47 percent of the respondents correctly identified the First*

Amendment to the Constitution as the document that guarantees
religious freedom to the American people. However, 32 percent
attributed the nation's commitment to religious freedom to the
Declaration of Independence, 9 percent thought the source was
the Ten Commandments, and 2 percent pointed to the Emancipation
Proclamation as the guarantor of our first freedom (First Freedom
Center, September 14, 2004).

- *Unfortunately, unless there are dramatic changes, prospects for*
  better future support of religious freedom are not good. The John S.
  and James L. Knight Foundation discovered that the First Amend-
  ment is "a second-rate issue" to many high school students nearing
  graduation. More than one in three of these students think the First
  Amendment goes "too far" in the rights it guarantees to American
  citizens (John S. and James L. Knight Foundation, January 31, 2005).

I have become convinced that, if put to a popular vote in a public referendum, the religious liberty clauses in the First Amendment
to the Constitution might not now be adopted.

The consequences of widespread misunderstanding and ignorance of religious liberty will alter the nature of our democracy;
compromise the integrity of religion; create a confused relationship
between religion, politics, and government; and set back the quality of interreligious relations and relationships between religion,
politics, and government to a degree that is detrimental to the nation. Something has to be done. Needed immediately are broad-
based programs of public education and keenly targeted initiatives
of activism related to a defense of religious liberty and its corollary—separation between the institutions of religion and government.

FIRST FREEDOM FIRST

In the summer of 2005, I met with Andy and Eva Grove along with
their daughter Karen Grove and Rebekah Saul Butler, program di-

rector at the Grove Foundation. During my visit with these visionary people, one that stretched across the better part of an afternoon, they expressed interest in initiating a public education campaign on the meaning and importance of religious freedom and its institutional counterpart of separation of church and state, and inquired as to whether or not The Interfaith Alliance Foundation, which I lead, would be interested in working on such an initiative. Needless to say, the possibility of embarking upon a well-financed campaign to reeducate America on religious freedom excited me beyond measure.

When the Groves inquired about another organization to be involved in this endeavor, I immediately suggested Americans United for Separation of Church and State (also referred to as Americans United or AU). The people at the Grove Foundation liked that idea. A few days later I talked with Barry Lynn, executive director of Americans United, about this initiative. Soon after, Barry visited with the Groves, and we started working on a plan.

What needed to be done? Over the years, Americans United for Separation of Church and State and The Interfaith Alliance Foundation have worked long and hard to address the problems that plague our Constitution's guarantee of religious freedom, and they have responded effectively to well-organized and richly funded attacks on this constitutional guarantee. But the work is neither easy nor inexpensive. Both of our organizations welcomed an opportunity to expand our outreach and to strengthen our work.

First, we wanted to educate people about the meaning and importance of religious freedom and to motivate them to become actively involved in its support. Second, we wanted to see the current issues essential to the preservation of religious freedom become a vital part of the national conversation, especially at times of heightened political discussions, such as presidential elections. Andy Grove passionately advanced the idea of securing thousands of signatures endorsing a petition that spelled out and affirmed the meaning of religious freedom. He envisioned presenting this petition to leaders of both political parties along with a call for them to help assure that religious freedom is a major topic of conversation during the next national elections. That vision is still in place and actions to make it a reality are in process.

In addition to prodding candidates for public office to talk about religious freedom, Andy, Barry, and I find great excitement in the possibility of millions of conversations among citizens who are interested in better understanding religious freedom and resolving to work relentlessly to strengthen it and protect it.

With great enthusiasm we launched a national public education campaign on religious freedom and separation of church and state under the title First Freedom First.

Religious freedom is often called our "first freedom." In the first session of the Continental Congress, the delegates' first fight was over faith. A lawyer from Boston, Thomas Cushing, moved that the session begin with prayer. Two other delegates immediately objected. Eventually, delegates reached a compromise that allowed an Episcopal clergyman to read a psalm at the beginning of the next day's session. Other battles of a similar nature ensued. And without question, the Continental Congress signaled its desire for a secular tone in political affairs alongside an appreciation for religion. As Jon Meacham observes in his book *American Gospel: God, the Founding Fathers, and the Making of a Nation,* the founders settled on a middle way and stayed the course—honoring religion's place in the nation while protecting religious freedom. Reflecting on the establishment of a new form of government, Meacham rightly praises the leaders for placing "the ideal and the reality of liberty and mutual understanding at the heart of the American tradition from the first year of the first presidency."

Religious freedom is now popularly known as our "first freedom" because it was the first freedom guaranteed by the United States Constitution and the freedom that formed the foundation on which other freedoms were constructed. Former Supreme Court justice Hugo Black called this first freedom "America's greatest gift to the world."

CONFUSION AND DEFINITIONS

Today, it is not enough for a person to declare, "I believe in religious freedom" or for an organization to announce that it supports religious freedom. Like so many other terms, these historic words have been hijacked by highly motivated people intent on destroying that which they claim to support. Right now, some people seek to withdraw freedom for everybody in order to claim freedom for themselves, in the name of religious freedom. A comment from President Taft about the Puritans is applicable to all such groups and individuals—"[They] came to this country to establish freedom of their religion, not the freedom of anybody else's religion."

Shortly after The Interfaith Alliance Foundation and Americans United for Separation of Church and State launched First Freedom First, the Family Research Council, a Religious Right organization, announced a program using the tagline "Defending Our First Freedom." Perhaps the Family Research Council's decision to use the "first freedom" terminology was a result of coincidence rather than an intention to link our First Freedom First campaign with its partisan political agenda. But a quick glance at the details of the organization's initiative quickly clarifies differences between its interest and ours. At a "Liberty Sunday" event in 2006, the Family Research Council aired a video "debunking" the traditional historical conclusion that most of the first European settlers in North America came to flee religious persecution and seek religious freedom. The Council's recommended alternative explanation for Europeans' initial immigration to this land was "The Lord Jesus had called them here, as . . . William Bradford put it, 'because they had a great hope and an inward zeal of advancing the cause of the gospel of the Kingdom of Christ in those remote parts of the earth.'" It is little wonder that Gary Bauer summoned that audience to recognize that "Our country was built on ordered liberty under God . . . liberty . . . tempered by virtue." By way of contrast, simply stated, at the heart of the First Freedom First campaign is an interest in democracy, not theocracy.

Surprisingly, during this same period of time, the United States Department of Justice also weighed in on liberty with a program called (can you believe it?) First Freedom Project. Consider this initiative within the context of the then Attorney General's positions and actions that have been hostile to religious freedom both prior to and subsequent to its launch: Rounding up Muslims for questioning simply because their religion is Islam and intruding into mosques are two examples. Failing to challenge government funding to religious organizations that have not adopted a legal status that places a firewall between government directives and religious authority, one that assures civil rights guarantees, is a third. Strengthening religious freedom for everybody—the goal of First Freedom First—differs dramatically from facilitating and justifying greater entanglement between the institutions of government and the institutions of religion.

When the subject is religious freedom, clarity is essential. Religious freedom has a specific meaning, not to be confused with a rhetoric of religious freedom that affirms freedom *for* but not *from* religion, or with a strategy for destroying the historic wall of separation between church and state. In the interest of such clarity, here are three definitions that can prove helpful to readers of this book —two related to the clauses in the First Amendment to the Constitution that assure religious freedom to all citizens of the United States, and one related to the movement that has imperiled religious freedom with its partisan and theocratic-leaning tactics.

The Establishment Clause

"Congress shall make no law
respecting an establishment of religion"

Succinctly stated, the first constitutional guarantee of religious freedom means that the government cannot make one religion preferable over another, or religion preferable over nonreligion in the nation. Every citizen has a right to expect that the government will remain neutral in matters of religion and that all citizens will enjoy equal rights and privileges regardless of their views on religion.

Applications of that guarantee prohibit the government from

subsidizing religion by providing public funds to houses of worship and/or pervasively sectarian organizations. It is also meant to prohibit any one or all three of the branches of government from promoting distinctively sectarian doctrines, values, and worldviews. Similarly, government is required to resist efforts of religious leaders and religious organizations to use the tools and other resources of the state to advance particular religious persuasions or values.

One of the best summaries of the meaning of the Constitution's Establishment was written as part of the 1947 Supreme Court majority opinion in the case of *Everson v. Board of Education of the Township of Ewing.* Using noninclusive language, Justice Hugo Black elaborated a comprehensive understanding of the Establishment Clause, asserting that it "means at least this: Neither a state nor the Federal Government can set up a church. Neither can pass laws which aid one religion, aid all religions, or prefer one religion over another. Neither can force nor influence a person [to] go to or remain away from church against his will or force him to profess a belief or disbelief in any religion. No person can be punished for entertaining or professing religious beliefs or disbeliefs, for church attendance or nonattendance." Drawing from Thomas Jefferson's letter to the Danbury Baptists, Justice Black concluded, "The First Amendment has erected a wall between church and state. That wall must be kept high and impregnable. We (the Supreme Court) could not approve the slightest breach."

The Free Exercise Clause

*"Congress shall make no law prohibiting
the free exercise thereof [of religion]"*

As a delegate to the state convention called to draft the Virginia Declaration of Rights in May of 1776, James Madison advocated for religious freedom. Madison was impressed with a line on freedom of religious expression written by George Mason—"all men should enjoy the fullest toleration in the exercise of religion"—but bothered by the word "toleration." After discussing with Patrick Henry his desire to move beyond the concept of merely allowing or permitting the exercise of religion, Madison secured the convention's embrace of his terminology—"all men are equally entitled to the free exercise of religion." The slight change in wording carried dramatic consequences. In *American Gospel,* Jon Meacham cites the scholarly observation of William Lee Miller, who pointed out that by accepting Madison's change of language in the Virginia Declaration of Rights adopted in June of 1776, the delegates took freedom of religion out of the category of "legislative grace" (which implies that what is granted can be rescinded) and affirmed it as "an inalienable right."

Framers of the First Amendment never intended mere tolerance of religion and certainly not a provision of freedom for religion that under certain circumstances could be removed. From the visionaries of our democratic experience came a promise that government was not to interfere with any person's freedom of religious expression. Every person was guaranteed an unlimited free exercise of religion up to the point that one individual's free exercise infringed upon another person's freedom of religious expression, or freedom to reject religion and all of its expressions.

The founders of our nation said "yes" to the free exercise of religion and "no" to any person impinging upon, compromising, or destroying another person's freedom. Likewise, citizens who do not embrace religion are free to express their humanism, secularism, or atheism as freely as others express their religion, and with the same boundary. The same principle applies to everybody. Any individual's free expression of commitment to religion or rejection of religion stops at the point at which it threatens or eradicates another individual's freedom of religion or freedom from religion.

"Congress shall make no law respecting an establishment of religion or prohibiting the free exercise thereof"

Every time I read or repeat these words, I am astounded by the vision and wisdom of those who wrote them. I know of no more perfect formula for regulating relationships between religion and government, one religion and other religions, and religious people and nonreligious people than the formula found in these clauses. No one has to worry about any specific religion, or religion generally, being established in a manner that makes nonadherents second-class citizens. Each person can practice his or her personal religion or rejection of religion with the assurance of freedom as long as such free expression does not deny the freedom of another person.

Reflecting on disagreements about the interpretation of these clauses while writing on a specific legal ruling, in *McCreary Country, Kentucky v. ACLU of Kentucky* in 2005, former United States Supreme Court justice Sandra Day O'Connor wrote, "The goal of the Clauses is clear: to carry out the Founders' plan for preserving religious liberty to the fullest extent possible in a pluralistic society. By enforcing the Clauses, we have kept religion a matter for the individual conscience, not for the prosecutor or the bureaucrat." Then, with reference to the violence around the world that has stemmed from governments assuming religious authority, Justice O'Connor wrote, "Americans may count themselves fortunate: Our regard for constitutional boundaries has protected us from similar travails, while allowing private religious exercises to flourish."

The Religious Right

References to the movement known as the Religious Right will appear repeatedly throughout this volume because it has been a primary source of major problems related to preserving religious freedom. Most important to keep in mind is the fact that the Religious Right is a *political*, not a religious, movement. Many members of the Religious Right assume that they are part of a religious movement strictly interested in promoting the moral values that they believe make the United States a better nation. But they are wrong. The Religious Right is not a homogenous movement. Indeed, the political operatives who lead Religious Right organizations often have motives, embrace strategies, and advance work toward goals that would not be shared by all of the people in the movement if rank and file members—often as well intended as they are misguided—knew what their leaders were doing.

Some people now refer to the Religious Right as the Christian Right. Such identification is understandable. However, members of the Religious Right include many participants whose interest is not religion and whose goal is not the moral rightness of the nation. Therefore, in this volume we will refer to this movement as the Religious Right.

The Religious Right began to take form in the 1970s as a result of the political activism of people like Pat Robertson and the organizational efforts of Rev. Jerry Falwell, who launched the Moral Majority. Today, new and multiple organizations lead the movement. Many would argue that Dr. James Dobson, president of the massive organization Focus on the Family, is the present leader of the Religious Right. However, Tony Perkins of the Family Research Council, Gary Bauer of American Values, Lou Sheldon of the Traditional Values Coalition, and Jay Sekulow, chief counsel of the American Center for Law and Justice, would argue that point. Then, too, many of the most influential voices now echoing the message of the Religious Right are politicians who embrace the kind of ideology forcefully articulated by Tom DeLay.

The Religious Right claims an interest in recovering morality in America by seeking to outlaw all abortions, stem cell research, gay rights, and same-sex unions while advocating the teaching of religious doctrine as sound science. They also advocate, through a system of school vouchers often lauded as a way to help the poor, providing public tax dollars for the funding of private parochial schools. In recent years, the Religious Right has been loud in its advocacy for advancing the president's faith-based initiatives, displaying the Ten Commandments in public buildings, teaching the Bible in public schools, electing "God-chosen" leaders to public offices, and supporting the president of the United States in speaking and acting as the chief religious leader of the nation. However, the Religious Right has been strangely silent on the war in Iraq, increases in the numbers of people without adequate medical care and health insurance, the torture of prisoners, invasions of privacy, a massive erosion of basic rights, and the need to strengthen both the Establishment Clause and the Free Exercise Clause in the First Amendment to the Constitution.

THREE VOICES, ONE MESSAGE

This book features the words of three different people. Each voice is distinct. The name of the pioneering scientist and innovative corporate executive Andy Grove is virtually synonymous with the amazing development of the Intel Corporation. In his preface, Andy writes with experience and passion about his concern for the deteriorating status of religious freedom and the separation of church and state in this nation. In his personal reflections, you will find echoes of the captivating story he told in his memoir *Swimming Across*—a narrative of his escape from Communist-controlled Hungary and his subsequent journey to America. Andy Grove will stir, challenge, and motivate all who read his comments on the constitutional assurance of religious freedom; to lose it would be to lose America.

Barry Lynn and I have worked together for almost two decades. We frequently share the same podium or sit together in front of a committee conducting a congressional hearing, each of us talking about religious freedom and the necessity of church-state separation. Because of Barry's legal training, in addition to his theological education, and my long years of serving as the pastor of several churches as well as working in the field of politics and religion, he and I typically deliver a one-two punch to proposed assaults on religious freedom. Barry speaks from the perspective of legality—the impact of violations of religious liberty on the Constitution—while I speak from the perspective of how such violations negatively impact the integrity of religion and threaten the vitality of democracy. Such are our respective approaches in this volume.

Andy, Barry, and I are different in many ways, but each of us lives with a resolve to protect and preserve the religious freedom and church-state separation promised by the United States Constitution. Now, challenged by the Religious Right and concerned that innumerable Americans are too uninformed about the dangers of losing this freedom to realize what they should be doing to protect it, the three of us have come together to write for education, persuasion, and inspiration. With one voice, we affirm the meaning and importance of our first freedom while pledging to give ourselves to the task of working in every possible venue to encourage, equip, and call to action people willing to support religious freedom as never before. We want to keep our first freedom first.

Part I: A Religious-Political Perspective

C. WELTON GADDY

Religious Freedom and the Success or Failure of Democracy

Recently, during breakfast with a highly respected public relations executive, the conversation turned to the subject of religious freedom. Almost immediately, through body language first and then in words, the woman expressed her disinterest in that topic. She explained that she was not "up" on religious issues because she cared little about religion. Needless to say, my breakfast partner was unmoved by my enthusiastic interest in the subject of religious freedom and its institutional requirement for separation between religion and government—at least initially.

As our conversation continued, our attention shifted to matters that were obviously of great interest to her. The woman spoke of her incredulity over opposition to embryonic stem cell research, her fear of the growing power of the Religious Right, and her dismay that mostly male religious leaders were seeking to deny reproductive rights to women. The longer she spoke, the more animated she became and the more forcefully words crossed her lips. At a proper moment, when she had paused to eat a spoonful of oatmeal, I pointed out that the two of us were still talking about religious freedom. Staring at me with a quizzical look on her face, she said, "I thought religious freedom just meant that we all have the freedom to decide where we will go to church or if we will attend church at all." "No," I responded, "religious freedom guarantees that no institution of government—at either the federal, state, or local level—can foist upon anybody the moral or doctrinal teachings of any one religion, or require by civil law personal conformity to a sectarian code of virtues. Religious freedom means that every person is free to make a decision about religion—to affirm, embrace, and practice religion privately and publicly or to reject religion as a matter of conscience and conviction." Now fully engaged in the conversation, and with her tone of voice indicating rising enthusiasm, the woman declared, "Now I do care about *that!*"

Unfortunately, my breakfast partner that morning represents a host of Americans who hold a narrow definition of religious freedom and thus do not recognize what is happening to the foundation of all freedoms in our nation. Scores of concerned citizens simply cannot or do not see the dynamic relationship between a myriad of social-political issues that they care about immensely, and worry about daily, to the two religious liberty clauses in the First Amendment of the United States Constitution.

Polling data consistently validate these observations. For example, right after President Bush launched his faith-based initiative in 2001, a Pew Research Center for the People and the Press poll found that 64 percent of the public supported a program of government funding for religious organizations involved in the provision of social services. However, the same poll found that when people understood that the faith-based model would come from the White House, only 46 percent thought it was a good idea (*Bush Approval on Par, No Tax Cut Momentum*, February 22, 2001). Similarly, members of the focus groups convened by Greenberg Quinlan Rosner Research on behalf of the First Freedom First campaign repeatedly declared strong support for religious freedom *and* strong antagonism, if not outright opposition, to the concept of church-state separation. Of those polled on this subject, 45 percent disagreed with the statement "There should be a high wall of separation between church and state" (Greenberg, Quinlan Rosner Research, December 8, 2006).

Such serious disconnects pose a grave danger to the ongoing strength of religious liberty. The public's failure to see the integral relationship between popular social-political issues and the impact of those issues on the status of religious freedom—government-funded religious activities, legislative attempts to impose sectarian values on the nation by means of government agencies, forced recitations of Christian prayers in public school classrooms, and government support for private religious schools, to cite only a few examples—jeopardizes responsible decision making, reduces the level of citizens' involvement in the legislative process, and weakens religious freedom.

Presently, neither political leaders nor religious leaders seem to care sufficiently about the strength of religious freedom to nurture it and protect it—just the opposite, really. Innumerable governmental and spiritual leaders alike send a strong message to the public that people had better embrace "the right kind of religion" or be treated as second-class citizens. And countless other citizens appear unwilling to challenge this worsening situation because they do not recognize the crucial role that this first freedom plays in American life.

Few people today realize the dire consequences of compromising, to say nothing of *losing*, the Constitution's guarantee of freedom of religion. "Oh, it's just a religion thing," some ill-informed individuals say with a yawn, shrugging their shoulders as if to say, "who cares?" Others view concerns about issues in church-state relations as inconsequential, not as "weighty" as other problems faced by American citizens. "Only the churches care about this issue," they say, calling conflicting views on religious liberty no more than an ideological debate of little relevance to the real problems that plague most citizens—taxes, medical care, elections, foreign policy, public education, and the like. Wrong! How dramatic is their misunderstanding. Few issues in the institutions of government now reside beyond the questions surrounding the proper role of religion in government and the proper influence of government on religion. Make no mistake about it; that debate powerfully impacts, and is impacted by, the "real problems" that revolve around and pulsate in issues such as taxes, medical care, elections, foreign policy, and public education. And the outcome of the debate about religious freedom is every bit as important as the debates about these "hot button" social-political issues and will be as consequential to people who hold no favor for religion as for those who do.

At stake in the fate of religious freedom is nothing less than the success or failure of democracy as envisioned and described in the United States Constitution and experienced by all citizens. In other words, the future of America's first freedom will determine to a great extent the future of the form of government and the way of life at the center of the vision that motivated and informed the founders of this nation. Should the moment ever arrive when Americans completely turn their attention away from the importance of religious liberty and cease to protect it vigorously, that will be the moment the fate of democracy hangs dangerously in the balance.

> "I have feared for years that Christianity, at least in the way it is interpreted by the evangelicals, would eventually remove all my civil freedoms that I have so fervently believed in all my life. . . . Religious freedom is the inalienable right to worship, or to not worship should that be the case, in any way in which I believe. The right to worship in a way that does not infringe on the rights of others while at the same time allowing me the right to practice my religion in a free and unhindered fashion. With so many people in the world still denied the freedom of religion, the freedom of worship, and the freedom of belief, the fact that I still currently have that right means everything to me. It is the true basis on which our country is founded, not on Christianity but on the freedom of religion."
>
> LISTENER, State of Belief

> "There is, actually, a test having to do with religion, and that is that the candidate upholds the First Amendment to the Constitution. Because the Religious Right is changing its meaning, we must inquire as to how their religion influences their interpretation of the First Amendment."
>
> MEMBER, Tulsa Interfaith Alliance

The Historical Foundation
of Religious Freedom

In the autumn of 2004 I had the privilege of speaking at a celebration of the two-hundred-and-seventy-fifth anniversary of Bedford, Massachusetts. Originally, the community that became the town of Bedford stretched between the towns of Billerica and Concord. However, getting to the meetinghouses in those two locations presented quite a challenge to residents of that community, especially during snowstorms. But participation in worship was not an option. Civil law in colonial Massachusetts mandated that a meetinghouse be accessible to every community and that all residents in a town attend the weekly services of public worship held in their town's meetinghouse. So in 1729, residents of the area between the towns of Billerica and Concord petitioned the state legislature to incorporate Bedford as a town. When that request was granted, a beautiful white frame building was constructed in the center of the town's square as the home of First Parish, the venue of the town's recent celebration of its incorporation.

Can you imagine governmental enforcement of required attendance in public worship? In Virginia, laws prohibited any consumption of food for a day among individuals who did not attend both morning and evening worship services on Sunday. The second time that people did not show up for worship, they were beaten. And the third time they were placed in prison for six months. Here is evidence of the disturbing truth that religious liberty has never been completely secure in this nation.

In fact, abuses of religious freedom abounded in colonial America. Religious assessments were levied against private citizens. Public tax dollars paid, in part, the salaries of ministers officially recognized by the government. Clergy in minority religious groups, like Baptists, did not receive financial support, though members of those minority traditions were required by law to pay money to help the government support the work of their government-endorsed colleagues. Quakers faired poorly in the colonies, in contrast to Anglicans, who, according to Thomas Jefferson, "retained full possession of the country about a century." For quite some time, most colonists refused to endorse a guarantee of freedom *from* religion as a complement to freedom *for* religion. And even freedom *for* religion was provided only for the majority-preferred religion. Civil officials in Virginia made it a crime for parents not to have their children baptized in the Anglican Church.

Several colonies required candidates for public office to pass a religious test. While in some colonies the test was as general as the candidate having to be a Christian, in other colonies the test was specific and doctrinal—the candidate had to be a Trinitarian Christian (one who believed in God as Father, Son, and Holy Spirit).

Christian laws—"Laws Divine, Moral and Martial"—not only mandated participation in public worship, but required citizens to exhibit behavior in conformity to Christian morals (Jon Meacham, *American Gospel*). The sin of adultery carried the death penalty, the same sentence that civil authorities in Connecticut imposed on people who worshiped any god other than the God Christians worshiped.

With the proposal of a Constitution that would move a new experiment in government from distinct and differing colonies to the "united states" of America, the relationship between religion and government took on national proportions. Important questions had to be resolved: Should each state retain a right to decide for itself about an established religion, religious tests for public office, and religious assessments through which all citizens supported government-sanctioned, publicly financed clergy? Would citizens be free from identification with and involvement in religion, or only free for an exercise of religion?

The Constitution that was adopted in 1787 answered only one of these questions. Article VI in that historic document forbids the application of a religious test for, or the imposition of a religious qualification on, candidates for public office. Many officials argued that answers to the other most important questions were implicit in the Constitution. But assurances in that regard were not sufficient for those minority religious leaders and other citizens who knew firsthand the public's capacity for intolerance toward people who did not share the majority religion, or held no religion at all.

"Dissenters," as these minority advocates were known—Unitarians, Baptists, Secularists, and Deists—pressed for an amendment to the United States Constitution that made religious freedom an unquestionable guarantee. Though the members of this coalition differed from each other dramatically in their views on the nature of religion and the value and place of religion in civil society, they spoke with one voice against the idea of a government-established national religion. Even Christian evangelicals who, as a part of their faith, longed for a Christian nation, understood that authentic religion was always a matter of choice and that without separation between the institutions of religion and the institutions of government, such a nation never could exist.

Finally, in response to this powerful grassroots movement to secure religious freedom, in 1789 the nation's founders placed the full force of the Constitution behind an assurance of religious freedom and a guarantee of the separation of church and state. They made religious freedom the foundation—the first freedom—upon which they constructed other freedoms and rights. Religious and nonreligious people alike understood the integral relationship between religious liberty and democracy, realizing that both require freedom for personal choices, deliberate decisions, and respect for differences.

In a haunting way, peering into the colonial past is not unlike looking carefully at the contentious present. Leaders of our early government had to find a way to satisfy both passionate evangelicals and aggressive secularists, to respect religion without endorsing it, and to make a place for voluntary religion in the nation without making an official place for it in the government. Wise leaders prodded by influential activists made it happen: the nation had a constitutional guarantee of religious freedom. But many people were not yet finished with attempts to make the government a servant of a particular religion, to impose the majority religion on minorities with little regard for their rights, and to make religion a test for candidates seeking public office. So much of then looks like now. So much of now looks like then.

Logic would suggest that, having noted potential dangers inherent in entanglements between the institutions of religion and the structures of government, and having learned important lessons from the necessity of colonial America's pursuit of religious freedom in its protection of democracy, contemporary America would spare itself the problems that accompany any erosion in religious liberty. One could reasonably surmise that having been forewarned about the tenuous status of this first freedom, contemporary Americans would be vigilant in rebuffing movements and events that, in weakening this constitutional guarantee, threaten as well the persistence of other civil rights and dimensions of freedom. Not so!

Since the late 1970s, while all of the previous challenges to religious freedom have persisted, new attacks on the historic wall of separation between institutions of government and religion have developed as well. Several new organizations that are unfriendly to the First Amendment have joined forces to form a movement of no little significance.

EMERGENCE AND GROWTH OF THE RELIGIOUS RIGHT

Many scholars consider the rise of the Religious Right in the latter part of the twentieth century the most important *political* development in recent history. Without question, the emergence of this movement has spawned a proliferation of problems related to religious freedom and church-state separation.

In the 1960s and early 1970s, mainline Christian churches in America, often joined by conservative and progressive Jewish congregations, amassed an impressive record of political involvement in support of civil rights legislation at home, and in opposition to the United States' involvement in the war in Southeast Asia. Martin Luther King, Jr. and his colleagues in the civil rights movement demonstrated the power of people of faith to organize, march, register voters, and influence officials at all levels of government. During this same time period, white evangelical Christians, as a group, continued to position politics beyond the purview of the church, espousing a cliché as a conviction—"Politics and religion don't mix." That, however, changed rather quickly.

Impressed by the successes of religious groups in achieving civil rights legislation and hastening the end of the war in Southeast Asia, observers saw the possibilities of achieving power and influence by organizing members of the conservative religious community. Power-oriented persons who combined political expertise with knowledge of the language of people of faith began to incite fears regarding an epidemic of immorality in the nation and the preeminence of secularism over "the one true faith." When popular, media-savvy religious leaders heralded the involvement of evangelical Christians in politics as the solution to these disturbing problems, scores of evangelicals responded positively to the call, quickly setting aside a disdain for politics to participate in a gaudy wedding of religion and politics.

Streetwise politicians, in turn, started to respond to the strong-arm tactics of this significant new, vocal, and hyperactive constituency known as the Religious Right. Some politicians decided to placate it and others decided to use it. Clergy people, who were as undiscerning about their engagement in political action as they had been about their former absence from it, pledged to deliver votes for candidates who were "ordained by God." Candidates for public office seeking such a lofty endorsement began to boldly speak the language of faith and aggressively appeal for the support of people of faith.

Two developments in particular highlight the danger this movement poses to religious freedom and the destructive impact of its almost daily assault on the historic wall of church-state separation.

It is little wonder that the public is confused about the meaning of religious freedom. That has been the intent of much of the Religious Right's initiative aimed at "debunking" religious freedom as promised in the Constitution.

First, the movement redefined religion. Just prior to the 2004 presidential election, on the set of a cable television network's evening news show in front of a national viewing audience, Rev. Jerry Falwell told me that he saw no way that any Bible-believing person could vote for anyone other than George W. Bush in the national presidential election. *How strange,* I thought. This noted pastor established a political criterion for passing judgment on another person's religion. Was it not the height of arrogance as well as heresy to judge the authenticity of a person's religion on the basis of that person's political preferences rather than on the person's confession of faith and commitment to a relationship with God?

Ah, but a redefinition of religion served well the purpose of seeking to win an election. And that was what was going on. Think of the voter pool that can be gathered for partisan causes when people eager to embrace real religion can be convinced that casting a vote for one particular candidate is synonymous with living a religious life. The whole thing is a terrible broadside against the integrity of religion, but it is a political strategy that seems to work, at least for now.

Second, the Religious Right narrowed the comprehensive concept of biblical morality to only four or five social-political issues, heralded as primal moral values. Strategically, politicians retained the rigidity of a fundamentalist mind-set but replaced their theological criteria for determining orthodoxy in belief with policy criteria for determining integrity in politics, patriotism in nationalism, and authenticity in spirituality. In the past, fundamentalist religious leaders determined who were "true believers" by inquiring about peoples' views on "the fundamentals"—the infallibility of the Bible, the historicity of miracles like the virgin birth, the "penal substitutionary" doctrine of atonement, and a realistic expectation of the second coming of Jesus. That changed. Holding "correct" political positions replaced believing orthodox religious doctrines as the criterion for determining true Christians. Religious Right leaders equated spiritual authenticity with a person's support for certain candidates for public office and advocacy for the "right" position on issues such as abortion, vouchers for public education, gay marriage, stem cell research, and public displays of the Ten Commandments.

The Religious Right has never been a homogenous movement. Rather, a few political operatives who understood religion, religious language, and houses of worship organized a diverse group of mostly well-meaning people who wanted little more than a better nation and manipulated them, their faith, and their religious institutions to advance a partisan political agenda. Once the first leaders of this movement stepped aside and Ralph Reed took control of the Christian Coalition in 1989, with every passing year, the Religious Right became larger, politically more astute, better financed, and more effective. After securing leadership positions in numerous state organizations of the Republican Party, the Religious Right forged a partnership with the national Republican Party. Politicians like Newt Gingrich found in the Religious Right organizing structures, communication networks, and more than enough volunteers to support programs like his Contract with America. Eventually, the merger of the Religious Right and the Republican Party brought about what Kevin Phillips calls, in his book *American Theocracy*, "the first religious party in the history of American politics."

Religious Right leaders built an impressive array of educational institutions for training young people in the skills needed to alter the way the nation does politics and interprets the Constitution. Under a pretense of advancing freedom, the Religious Right took dead aim at delegitimizing church-state separation and redefining the meaning of religious freedom.

Perhaps nothing better illustrated the importance assigned to the Religious Right by high government officials than the White House calling James Dobson, president of the Religious Right organization Focus on the Family, to notify him of whom the president would nominate as an associate justice of the United States Supreme Court—before this information was provided to the United States Senate. Even as this book goes to press, presidential hopefuls within the Republican Party are wooing Religious Right leaders to gain their endorsements and backing during the upcoming presidential campaign.

The Religious Right has made a prominent place for itself on the religious-political landscape of this nation. No laws have been broken. No coup occurred. Skilled people simply strategically manipulated religious leaders and organizations to accomplish their political purposes. A proliferation of court cases aimed at altering the meaning of religious liberty reflects the effectiveness of this movement, and will be discussed later in this book.

Of course, members of the Religious Right have every right to speak their minds and advocate for their causes. My opposition to this movement, however, is based on the Religious Right's exclusionary form of government and intolerance of the religious pluralism and secular diversity supported by the First Amendment to the Constitution. The Religious Right is in order in summoning supporters, but out of order in wanting to alter the First Amendment to the Constitution so that once again a religious majority can control access for minority religious groups or people who embrace no religion. Based on a myriad of personal experiences with its leaders and assaults from them, I have concluded that the Religious Right is bad for religion, dangerous to democracy, oppressive in society, and a source of deep divisions within our nation.

To my astonishment, recently some people have begun to declare that the Religious Right is dead. Though this may make you feel better, do not be fooled. The anticipated funeral for the Religious Right has no corpse. The movement is alive and changing. A new generation of Religious Right leaders is appearing with the same old complaints but with revised and more effective strategies for success.

"RELIGIOFICATION" OF POLITICS
AND POLITICIZATION OF RELIGION

Once evangelical Christians removed the stigma they traditionally had attached to politics and embraced political activity as a form of Christian ministry, political action among conservative Christians took on the appearance and generated the enthusiasm of mass evangelism. The result has been a huge mobilization of people eager to Christianize America—its culture, politics, and government—that assaults the very foundations of freedom and seeks to rearrange the relationship between the institutions of religion and the institutions of government envisioned in the Constitution. Given the close relationship between democracy and religious liberty I mentioned earlier, this movement that threatens the status of religious liberty also threatens the strength of American democracy.

Nowhere are attempts at a new arrangement between religion and government more apparent than on the campaign trails that crisscross the nation during national elections, in the legislative agenda of conservative religious institutions, and in efforts to alter judicial opinions related to the meaning of religious freedom in the United States Constitution.

On the campaign trail

Aware of the public's interest in religion and the large number of potential voters resident in the constituency of the Religious Right, and attentive to directions offered by leaders of that movement, politicians seeking public office began using, and continue to manipulate, religion as a campaign strategy. "God bless America" has become a phrase considered as patriotic as it is religious. "God's candidate for this hour" have become manipulative words of partisan political endorsement spoken by religious leaders supporting a particular candidate for public office. Political strategists for both Democrats and Republicans schedule their respective candidates for visits to houses of worship, mostly churches, as conscientiously as they do to the conventions of America's unions, VFW assemblies, and meetings that bring together their respective "bases." A person's choice of candidate for the presidency has become a reflection of that person's religion. Not only are states considered "blue" or "red" depending upon the presidential candidate who won the majority of popular votes, but even churches have taken on "blue" or "red" identities.

In the 2004 presidential campaign, unprecedented steps were taken to turn houses of worship into campaign agencies. In June of that year, the Bush-Cheney '04 Campaign launched an effort to identify "1600 Friendly Churches" in Pennsylvania. In the e-mail to advance this program, leaders of houses of worship were asked to identify someone within each of their respective congregations to serve as a liaison with the Bush-Cheney Campaign. (Listed as the sender of the June 1, 2004, e-mail was GeorgeW-Bush.com/BushCheney04@GeorgeWBush.com. The subject line read "Lead Your Congregation for President Bush.") The purpose of this initiative was to do partisan political organizing within houses of worship—to utilize houses of worship to elect Mr. Bush and Mr. Cheney respectively to the offices of the presidency and the vice presidency of the nation. One month later, the Bush-Cheney '04 Campaign distributed by fax (July 1, 2004) the duties of a "Coalition Coordinator" in a local church, which included responsibilities such as: "Send your Church Directory to your State Bush-Cheney '04 headquarters" or give it to a field rep of the campaign; "Identify another conservative church in your community who can organize for Bush"; and "Finish calling all Pro-Bush members of your church and encourage them to vote."

What utter disdain for the sanctity of houses of worship! What a blatant broadside against the spirit and intent of the First Amendment! I find little comfort in the fact that on October 8, 2004, the Bush-Cheney '04 Campaign faxed scores of press releases entitled "Constitutional Attorney Jay Sekulow Calls on Kerry Campaign to Halt Illegal Campaign Activity in Churches." The nerve!

Look carefully at this picture. The administration that, as one of its first priorities, established an Office of Faith-Based and Community Initiatives in the White House sought to establish political offices in houses of worship in its bid for reelection. The nation needs neither. Both were affronts to the hard-won victory that established religious liberty in this land and guaranteed an institutional separation between religion and government, including partisan politics. Such campaign tactics cloud the public's understanding of religious freedom and commend an abuse of religion that compromises the independence and integrity of religion.

In the halls of Congress

Even a quick glance at the legislative agenda of the Religious Right and its adherents raises questions about the security of religious liberty. Concerns intensify with awareness of the alarming openness of this agenda displayed by members of the United States Congress. Let me be specific.

During the 109th Congress of 2005 and 2006, with a Republican majority resident in both houses, the undue influence of the Religious Right was apparent in an attempt to pass a federal marriage amendment and to fast-track confirmation of judicial nominations. Primarily because of the influence of the Religious Right, the Republican majority was willing to force a vote on the proposed marriage amendment despite the fact that they knew its passage had no chance. Passage, however, was not the point. The Religious Right knew that advocacy for this issue would significantly rally its base. The Republicans were well aware of their need for such a development as a means of bolstering support for their party in the upcoming election.

The influence of the Religious Right on the way Congress responded to judicial nominations was more dramatic in its politicking and had even more far-reaching consequences. A succinct summary of this effort coupled with one example of its success will suffice to make the point.

In April of 2005, Tony Perkins of the Family Research Council, Dr. James Dobson of Focus on the Family, Dr. Al Mohler of the Southern Baptist Theological Seminary, and Chuck Colson of Prison Fellowship Ministries launched a campaign to get conservatives appointed to the United States Supreme Court and hundreds of other federal courts. The right advanced the message of this initiative as "Justice Sunday: Stop the Filibuster Against People of Faith."

Through this much-hyped campaign, the Religious Right sought to undo two hundred years of established rules that protect the rights of the minority party and prevent the nation's courts from being overrun with biased judges. Devotees of the right worked hard to secure rules changes that would deny any senator the right to challenge judicial nominees, thus eliminating a senator's ability to act with accountability in responding to the will of constituents.

Had the right succeeded in securing all the changes it sought, members of the United States Senate would have lost the right to stand up to President Bush's (or any future president's) most biased nominees whose political and judicial agendas clearly threatened civil rights and religious liberties. The very nature of the Senate would have been altered as the right tightened its grip on the courts, took the air out of democracy, and further solidified the likelihood of its control of the judiciary in the nation for years to come.

Behind the Religious Right's well-organized political activism related to judicial nominees, Pat Robertson was praying for God's assistance in this endeavor. In a message posted on Robertson's Web site, the media mogul brazenly asked his followers to pray for God to remove three justices from the Supreme Court. "Would you join with me and many others in crying out to our Lord to change the Court?" Robertson wrote, "One justice is 83 years old, another has cancer, and another has a heart condition.... With their re-tirement and the appointment of conservative judges, a massive change in federal jurisprudence can take place."

The Religious Right's efforts have worked; or, at least they appear to be working. President Bush accommodated the legislative and judicial agenda of the Religious Right. He has done his part to change the nature of church-state relations in the nation for years to come.

When President Bush nominated his White House lawyer, Harriet Miers, to replace Sandra Day O'Connor as a justice on the

Supreme Court, protest from the Religious Right, questioning Ms. Miers's conservative credentials, was immediate, strong, well coordinated, and successful. Within a month the president withdrew the Miers nomination due to lack of congressional support. The president named as Miers's replacement Samuel Alito, the man whose nomination eventually received confirmation. The Religious Right found Alito worthy of the nomination and acceptable as a guardian of its agenda. Already, Justice Alito and Chief Justice John Roberts have helped swing the Court to the right on a series of issues including abortion, the White House Office of Faith-Based and Community Initiatives, free speech, and racial segregation.

Please keep in mind that all of this activity was done legally and with the consent of a majority of American voters. The Religious Right simply flexed its muscles powerfully and effectively and members of Congress responded agreeably.

After the 2006 elections, the Democratic takeover of the 110th Congress did not erase the substantive influence of the Religious Right on Capitol Hill. A more recent, prime example of the right's still-strong influence was the pressure exerted on Congress to uphold President Bush's veto of stem cell research legislation. On the checklist of the right, that box is marked "Done."

This is some of the background on what has transpired to bring us to this critical moment in which we are contemplating a dramatic reversal of the institutional relationship between religion and government as defined by the First Amendment to the Constitution. We did not get here quickly, but that does not mean that we cannot see history reversed with all deliberate speed. First, though, there is a question that deserves to be answered.

HOW COULD THIS HAPPEN?

Historical amnesia

Distance from a crisis alters people's sense of urgency regarding the danger of a repetition of it. Two hundred and sixteen years have passed since the visionary founders of this nation responded to the crisis of a lack of guaranteed religious freedom. Between that time and the present, many people have lost sight of the dangers of living without religious liberty.

The pressure of what is desired in the present moment distracts any focus on long-range consequences of certain political actions. For example, the faith-based initiative requires that recipients of faith-based services effectively give up their civil rights. No one will say that up front, but that is the long-term consequence of the program. When religious entities are granted exemptions from basic civil rights guarantees, people in need of social services may be forced to listen to a sermon, to attend a class of religious education, or to deny their sexual orientation in order to get help.

When religious entities become dependent upon government money, seldom do their leaders have the courage to challenge the government's wrongdoing. It seems better to get money for a ministry than to risk the loss of that money by raising questions or making charges related to the morality of business and government no-bid contracts, preemptive military strikes against another nation, the torture of prisoners, or burgeoning domestic problems in the areas of education, health care, and energy. Religious leaders who accept government subsidies to fund their ministries, thus becoming contract employees of federal agencies, seldom want to be prophetic and risk their employer being offended enough to cut off funding!

Far too few people are aware that a majority of the immigrants who gave shape to America's colonial government still preferred a majority religion supported by everyone's tax dollars and restrictive to the rights of minorities. This arrangement gave birth to problems that were prolific and powerful enough to disrupt the citizenry and threaten democracy. Surely, we do not want to go there again.

Historical amnesia fosters contemporary blindness when it comes to dangers threatening religious freedom. Unaware of the past, people see and condemn abuses of freedom and religion in foreign lands—even nations whose names carry a reference to a single religion—but remain blind to the relevance of such dangerous trends in the United States.

A lack of civic education

Several generations of Americans have grown into adulthood unaware of how our government functions in general, and specifically why separation between institutions of government and of religion is so important. Polling data paint a frightening picture of the level of the public's understanding of religious freedom and of the declining interest in protecting freedom, particularly among young Americans.

During the 2004–2005 school year, the John S. and James L. Knight Foundation conducted a wide-ranging survey of 112,003 high school students around the country seeking data related to the future of the First Amendment. The findings of this polling were far from comforting. A whopping 37 percent of the students did not even know about the First Amendment, 36 percent said they take it for granted, and only 27 percent indicated they even think about it. Equally disturbing, 21 percent of the students did not know what rights the First Amendment guarantees. But, of those who were aware of the content of the First Amendment, as mentioned in the introduction, 35 percent thought the Constitution "goes too far" in the rights it guarantees. Less that half of those surveyed, 44 percent of the high school students, approved of the rights guaranteed in the First Amendment.

Recently, a former associate justice on the United States Supreme Court expressed her dismay at the lack of civic education received by young people in the nation. Justice Sandra Day O'Connor pointed to the National Constitution Center's discovery that more teenagers can name the Three Stooges than can name the three branches of the United States government (*Washington Post*, June 27, 2007, H1).

Misinformation related to religious freedom

Sadly, I must report that not all of the misunderstanding that surrounds religious freedom or desensitization about its importance comes from disinterest, or neglect of the subject. Huge amounts of money and energy have been devoted to convincing the American public that they have been misinformed about the meaning and importance of religious freedom. A case in point is the work of the revisionist historian David Barton and his organization called Wall Builders. The name of Barton's organization raises constitutional red flags about its mission. Since Barton believes that the separation of church and state is a myth recently created by liberal Supreme Court justices, one might assume that the name of his organization would be Wall Destroyers. But the conservative juggernaut moving through our nation has adopted the strategy of describing its mission with language that presents an image that is directly contradictory to its mission—thus, Wall Builders. At the center of Barton's work is the notion that the United States was founded, and should be governed, as a Christian nation.

Couple these disturbing realities with the following influential social-political developments and you see with even greater clarity the disaster toward which we are moving unless we make a major course correction.

A growing diversity of religions in the nation has stoked the fires of majoritarianism

According to Diana Eck's studies of the "new religious America," the United States is now the most religiously diverse nation in the world. All of the major religions and countless minor ones now reside in this nation. Christianity remains the dominant religion (claiming over 250 million believers) but other religions have a sizable presence, often exerting an influence disproportionate to the number of their adherents. The United States is home for at least 4 million Muslims (more Muslims than Episcopalians or Presbyterians). Jews in the United States number around 4 million. There are at least 2.4 million Buddhists in this land (some estimate there are as many Buddhists as Jews), a million Hindus, a half-million Unitarian Universalists, 130,000 Baha'is (one of the fastest growing faiths in the United States), about 50,000 Native American religionists, and 50,000 Scientologists.

The boards I work with personally are made up of Christians, Hindus, Buddhists, Jews, Unitarians, Muslims, and Sikhs. The organizations I lead have 185,000 members who come from over seventy-five different religious traditions.

Religious diversity confronts our nation with a terrific challenge. Typically, increasing levels of abuse, conflict, and violence emerge when religious bodies do not practice mutual respect for each other and commit themselves to working together. Here is where a commitment to religious freedom makes such a positive difference for good in the nation. Religious liberty prohibits one religion from seeking to establish itself as *the* official religion of the nation—posting its scriptures in public institutions, funding its ministries from the federal treasury, and using public schools to teach its beliefs and practices. More positively, religious liberty encourages and provides security for people with diverse, even contradictory, views about religion to cooperate with each other and to do the work of democracy together without fearing that one will attempt to diminish another's freedom or competing with one another to secure the favoritism or endorsement of government.

Viewed from the perspective of the radical diversity that characterizes our nation, the religious freedom provision of the founders is astounding in its relevance, methodology, and effectiveness in the present moment. I know of no arrangement that could be more helpful for such radical religious diversity than that defined by the First Amendment to the United States Constitution: first, no established religion—that is, no official endorsement of one religion over others or of religion over nonreligion—and second, everyone free to practice religion or not to practice religion according to the dictates of conscience, up to the point that one person's free expression does not infringe upon or compromise another person's freedom. However, some people who are frightened by religious diversity are also threatened by religious liberty.

Frankly, the fact that a growing number of different religions are calling America home is calling many citizens' bluff regarding their previously professed loyalty to the constitutional guarantee of no establishment of religion—the prohibition of the government elevating one religion over another or religion over nonreligion. My hunch is that in the past, many people supported the Establishment Clause of the Constitution so enthusiastically because they presumed a practical establishment of religion in this nation—the religion of Christianity. Now these people feel threatened. A Hindu chaplain has led an opening prayer for a session of the United States Senate. A Muslim has been elected to the United States House of Representatives, repeating his oath of office with one hand on a copy of the Qur'an. A member of Congress has openly discussed his lack of a theistic faith and his devotion to humanism. The Department of Transportation continues to train employees in how to deal with Sikhs who wear turbans through security screening machines. Presidents Bill Clinton and George W. Bush have invited minority religious groups to the White House to honor celebrations of their primary religious festivals.

People disturbed by these developments do not disavow the Establishment provision guaranteed by the Constitution. They simply speak and behave *as if* their religion is the established religion. Typically, such people refuse to acknowledge even the presence, much less the rights and importance, of other religions in their communities. Is the opinion of the country's religious majority to dominate once again?

Even two Supreme Court justices—Antonin Scalia and Anthony Kennedy—have indicated that religious liberty controversies should perhaps be resolved by majority opinions in local communities rather than by Court decisions aimed at protecting minority rights. In a 2003 Religious Freedom Day speech (how ironic) in Fredericksburg, Virginia, and two years earlier (January 29, 2001) in a debate in Honolulu, Hawaii, Justice Scalia advocated that legislation, not Court decisions, determine the resolution of controversies about religious freedom. Imagine the consequences of such a strategy for guaranteeing religious freedom evenhandedly across the country. What happens to the protection of minority religions, and to people with no religion, if religious freedom becomes contingent upon a majority vote in a local community?

In his ruling on the legality of a nativity scene in a county court-house, *Allegheny County v. ACLU,* Justice Kennedy said local communities should decide about the appropriateness of displays on religious holidays. Has Justice Kennedy forgotten about religious diversity and minority rights in this nation? Consensus on a religious holiday display in a small village may be possible in some regions of the country, but how does a constitutionally fair decision get made in New York City, or Louisville, Kentucky, or thousands of other religiously diverse communities in our nation?

Equally problematic for religious liberty and for democracy is the philosophy that religious liberty is a states' rights issue. Supreme Court justice Clarence Thomas speaks of the First Amendment's Establishment Clause as no more than a "federalism provision." Thomas takes the position that, though the federal government cannot establish a national religion, states are free from the prohibition against an establishment of religion. Imagine what would happen to the cooperation amid diversity made possible by religious liberty and democracy if every one of the fifty states established its own official religion!

The Fourteenth Amendment to the Constitution expressly forbids states from taking actions that deprive citizens of equal protection under the law. Subsequently, the high court addressed this matter for purposes of even greater clarity, specifically incorporating the Free Exercise Clause and the Establishment Clause in 1940 and 1947, respectively. State governments cannot override the freedom of religion assurance provided in the Bill of Rights of the Constitution. Why would a justice of the Supreme Court even want to try to eliminate this guarantee of our first freedom?

Mushrooming societal needs have stirred compassion and blinded the public's vision regarding the importance of separation between the institutions of religion and government

The money made available by President Bush's wrongly conceived and ill-advised faith-based initiative looks so good and appears to be so helpful to people singularly interested in feeding the hungry and rehabbing drug addicts that they do not even consider the long-term consequences of houses of worship becoming receptacles for federal funds, and thus contractual employees of the federal government. The president has explained repeatedly that he wants federal funds to go to faith communities because faith is the factor that makes their social service programs more effective than those of secular agencies. In my head, I ask our leader, "Whose faith, Mr. President—mine, yours, or the faith of someone else? And what business is it of the government to be funding religious education?" Regardless of the answer to that question, the Constitution is clear: government has no business funding faith, using tax dollars to support religious programs.

Here, as few other places, the extent of deterioration in the nation's appreciation for church-state separation is so apparent. Contrast two developments, one contemporary and one early in our nation's history.

In 2001, President Bush announced that he would make government funding for social programs offered by religious organizations one of the hallmarks of his administration. No sooner was he in the Oval Office than the president established the White House Office of Faith-Based and Community Initiatives. For the first time in the nation's history, taxpayers' money flowed directly into the coffers of sectarian organizations.

In 1811, President James Madison vetoed a bill passed by Congress to authorize government funds to go to a church in Washington, D.C., to support its efforts to help the poor. Madison understood both religion and the Constitution. He was of the opinion that subsidizing religion even for such a noble task would jeopardize the First Amendment's guarantee of religious freedom. Madison explained to Congress that he vetoed the law because it "would be a precedent for giving to religious societies, as such, a legal agency in carrying into effect a public and civil duty."

What a difference exists between the thought of Madison and Bush! Unfortunately, President Bush seems to reflect in both thought and deed the serious drift away from the religious liberty guarantees of the Constitution that characterizes much of the American public. Such is the dangerous result of historical amnesia, misinformation about religious freedom, lack of civic education, fear of diversity, and bias toward majoritarianism in thoughts about both religious liberty and democracy.

What Now? A Strategy for Strengthening Religious Liberty

No sooner had immigrants to the North American continent set foot on its shoreline, fleeing from the intolerance and persecution characteristic of the established church in their European homes, than they began to reproduce here the religious discrimination, religious persecution, and myriad of abuses of religious freedom that they had fled. Today, faced by runaway pluralism and an approach to government that erases the distinction between religion and politics, people seek the will of the majority at the expense of the rights of minorities. Opposition to the constitutional guarantee of no establishment of religion has increased. Some citizens who affirm freedom for religion are not willing to concede a guarantee of freedom from religion.

Whether looking into the mirror of the nation's colonial history or through a window at the currents in contemporary America, when it comes to religious liberty the view is similar. Three disturbing realities raise the important question of what should be done next.

First, the stark reality is that, in every age, the psyche of the majority seems to swing away from concerns for the rights of minorities even if the majority has formerly experienced hardships as a minority. Thus, the security of religious liberty is in question once again.

Second, in every era of American history, perceptive students of religion and government have understood that the right of religious liberty and the rights that constitute political freedom are integrally related. One could argue that the ratification of the First Amendment was as much about preserving the democratic vision as about establishing religious freedom. It was both, of course. But one without the other always seemed to be in jeopardy. Today, the two—religious liberty and rights essential to a democracy—remain interrelated, but people prize security more than liberty and are willing to compromise both. At times, it appears that freedom has almost become a bad word. In such an environment, our first freedom is threatened.

The third reality takes the form of an observation. To lose religious freedom as guaranteed in the First Amendment to the Constitution would be, at the same time, to lose the form of government embraced throughout the Constitution. Citizens who fail to see the value of religious liberty on its own merits surely should be cognizant of and awakened to action because of the fact that the nature of democracy is violated without this freedom.

So here is the question: what comes next? More to the point, what should we do?

People in colonial America had a plan for responding to a crisis related to religious liberty in their time. A diverse coalition of activists took on the challenge of amending the Constitution with a guarantee of religious freedom. Today, the subject needs the attention of activists again—activists who will form a broadly based, diverse coalition to protect the constitutional guarantee secured by our predecessors.

A TO-DO LIST

Work is required on three fronts. First, educating the public regarding the meaning and importance of religious liberty is a prerequisite to the other two components in a sound strategy for action. Second, strengthening religious liberty requires strengthening democracy. And third, the work of protecting religion will bring to the coalition diverse people, even nonreligious people, interested in protecting religious freedom. The success or failure of this strategic work will powerfully impact, for good or ill, the nature of government as we have experienced it up to now.

Educating the public

Democracy functions best with an informed citizenry. Indeed, Thomas Jefferson repeatedly linked the success of democracy with quality education for the citizenry. It is no wonder that public education accessible to everybody was a priority among governmental leaders seeking to mature an infant democracy.

The principle involved here is not a dated one. In his best-selling book, *Cultural Literacy*, E. D. Hirsch writes, "Having the right to vote is meaningless if a citizen is disenfranchised by illiteracy or semiliteracy."

Earlier I mentioned former associate justice Sandra Day O'Connor's concerns about the lack of understanding of our judiciary among young people. Since her retirement from the Supreme Court, O'Connor has been a strong voice of support for education that turns good students into good citizens. Drawing on research done by the Carnegie Corporation and the Center for Information and Research on Civic Learning and Engagement, O'Connor has asserted that, generally speaking, today's students do not receive the educational foundation needed to become good citizens. Recently, Justice O'Connor pointed her finger directly at the current approach to teaching civics and called it a problem that must be overcome in the interest of transforming students into good citizens.

Justice O'Connor urged that civics curricula include historical references to specific incidents in which active civic participation contributed to the strengthening of democracy. She also insisted on problem-based learning in which students are drawn into the democratic process to address issues of interest to them, and Web-based learning that involves interactive civic participation. Justice O'Connor's plea for education in citizenship is true to the insistence of democratic leaders throughout our history. Perhaps that is why she concluded her article by observing, "The Framers would expect no less of us" (*Washington Post,* June 27, 2007, H5).

All that is written above about civic education is generally applicable to education about religious liberty specifically. People who understand the meaning of religion, the meaning of freedom, and the nature of democracy are more likely to actively protect religious liberty.

Presently, obedience to that educational imperative necessitates, at least in part, getting rid of misunderstanding—intentional on the part of some—in order to promote understanding of the substance of religious freedom.

Eradicating myths

I had looked forward to the occasion—fifteen executive-level experts in marketing and public relations who had agreed to work with The Interfaith Alliance Foundation on messaging. When I walked into the room and saw these people sitting at a circular oak table, pens in hand, legal pads in front of them, I took a deep breath and resolved to enjoy as well as to learn from this session.

"Why are you hostile to religion?" That was the first question, posed with a bit of disdain.

"We are not hostile to religion," I responded, "Just the opposite, actually. That is why we seek to protect the integrity of religion as well as the vitality of democracy; we want religion to act like religion and do its work with strength as well as credibility."

Quickly, the first questioner spoke again, displaying his embrace of the as-popular-as-it-is-destructive myth that support for religious freedom is an expression of hostility toward religion. Advancing such myths is integral to the strategy aimed at eliminating the influence of people who support religious freedom and the institutional separation of religion and government.

Reality presents problems enough for those of us committed to protecting and strengthening religious liberty and guaranteeing the separation of institutions of religion and institutions of government. Mythology perpetrated as history makes this work even more difficult. The fact that some people intentionally spread harmful myths is an aggravation to be endured as well as an unpatriotic form of troublemaking that needs to be exposed for what it is—a bending of truth to advance sectarian-oriented politics.

Naiveté is dangerous. Even myths that are laughable to those who know American history can ultimately jeopardize freedom. We had better take seriously a mythology that already has taken a heavy toll on the public's support for religious liberty. Indeed, eradicating popular myths is as essential as espousing unpopular truths. Four widely discussed myths invite responses that have the power to destroy them.

Myth: Support for church-state separation
is an expression of hostility toward religion

This fallacious assertion—which I encountered even in a room filled with highly educated and well-trained executives—is the product of either brainwashing of the American public inflicted by the Religious Right, an initiative of political strategy, or ignorance born of deficiency in the basic lessons of civics.

Many people simply do not recognize the importance of the untruth at the heart of this piece of attack-by-falsehood. But even more people—well-intentioned people—fall victim to the power of this deceitful message perpetrated as a political strategy.

The reasoning behind advancing this myth can be seen quickly and clearly once a person discovers the purpose it serves. Think about this: if a constitutional guarantee stands in the way of a desired sectarian or partisan political action, change the meaning of the guarantee or amend the Constitution and you gain acceptance for the action. On this matter, the Religious Right chose the easier course. They simply worked to change people's understanding of the Constitution. Unfortunately, scores of citizens were so uneducated on the meaning of religious freedom that this tactic worked effectively.

The Religious Right took dead aim at discrediting the validity of Thomas Jefferson's metaphor of "a wall of separation between church and state." Alarmists took to their religious pulpits and political stumps, claiming that the wall of separation forbids people from bringing the beliefs and values of their religion into their civic life. That is not the case at all! Institutional separation between religion and government is not synonymous with divorcing religion and government in personal citizenship. But the strategy of misinformation worked with alarming effectiveness.

In the introduction, I cited statistics showing the result of this misinformation campaign. More such findings emerged from polling done by The Interfaith Alliance and Americans United for Separation of Church and State in 2005, as we prepared for the launch of our First Freedom First campaign. Focus groups told us what language best conveyed the meaning of the religious liberty clauses in the First Amendment to the Constitution. However, many of the people who affirmed religious freedom opposed reference to and emphasis on church-state separation. Individuals who considered religious freedom an important part of the Constitution spoke of church-state separation as a tool of people negative toward religion. The power of myth!

Though the actual words "a wall of separation between church and state" do not appear in the Constitution, no question exists about the importance of those words for understanding the meaning and application of the words related to religion in the Bill of Rights. Jefferson, like most of the founders of the nation, knew firsthand that entanglement between the institutions of religion and government spelled trouble for both religion and government.

Actually, neither the word "church" nor the words "wall of separation" appear in the Constitution. To be sure, Jefferson's metaphor was never meant to apply religious liberty only to Christian churches or to erect a barrier that would restrict individuals' religion from interacting with decision making in the civil arena. My friend Gene Garman, author of *America's Real Religion*, insists that paying close attention to Jefferson's metaphor is a prerequisite to correctly understanding religious liberty. Garman uses phraseology that is rhetorically more cumbersome than Jefferson's, and thus

less effective in public relations efforts, but definitively more ac-
curate in important distinctions. Garman advocates usage of the
phrase "separation between the institutions of religion and the institutions of government." Obviously, Garman's language has influenced me. Because of my heavy involvement in multireligious
work, this terminology appeals to my sensitivities, and I have used
it repeatedly here. Nobody should have any doubt that religious
freedom is constitutionally guaranteed to mosques, gurdwaras,
temples, shrines, and synagogues, as well as to churches and to
people totally disinterested in any of these places of worship and
meditation.

Garman's language also makes the point that, regarding religious liberty, what is understandable and acceptable individually
is impermissible institutionally. Stated in another manner, what
the Constitution forbids institutionally is not forbidden personally.
Individuals invariably bring to their involvement in government
beliefs and values born and nurtured by their religions or their
nonreligious ideologies. But any entanglement between religious
institutions and government institutions is bad news for the Constitution, a problem for religion, and a serious threat to government
by democracy.

Those who pursue intercourse between institutional expressions of religion and government seem to have forgotten that the
children of that union always hurt true religion and leave no room
for, much less respect for, nonreligious people or any religion other
than the one in bed with the government.

The terminology, "separation of church and state" has long communicated the kind of distance needed between institutional expressions of religion and government. That meaning must be
recovered lest the government take on the identity of the church,
or the mosque take on the role of the government, or religion and
government become so confused that one cannot distinguish politics, religion, and government, nor presidents from pastors, nor
political leaders from religious leaders. To this day, the Queen of
England (now often in consultation with her prime minister) ap-
points the Archbishop of Canterbury, the ecclesiastical superior

who oversees the Anglican Church worldwide. This is not separation of church and state. This is the kind of arrangement Jefferson opposed.

In the present environment, those who most disdain the terminology of separation of church and state are the loudest advocates for using legislation to impose sectarian values on the American public, using a religious test for candidates for public office, and securing government subsidies for religious ministries. This, too, is the kind of arrangement Jefferson opposed, as do all who want to protect and strengthen religious liberty.

*Myth: The Constitution guarantees freedom
for religion but not freedom from religion*

How can so many people in the Religious Right express support for religious freedom when so much of their thought contradicts the basic principles of religious freedom and so many of their actions are prohibited by the constitutional promise of religious freedom? Here is how that works. If a fight over an issue cannot be won straightforwardly, one tried-and-true tactic is to change the meaning of the issue at the center of disagreement and frame it in a manner that ensures victory. Such a strategy seems apparent as Religious Right leaders speak about religious liberty. More and more, speakers affirm religious liberty by arguing that the Constitution guarantees freedom for religion but not freedom from religion.

In the summer of 2000, Marvin Olasky published the definitive statement on compassionate conservatism, the name of a philosophy that he made the title of his book. Then Texas governor George Bush wrote the foreword to Olasky's book, praising his recommendations incorporating compassion into government. Not far into his book, Olasky observes that the wall of separation of church and state "would stop compassionate conservatism in its tracks if it were part of the Constitution," adding: "But it's not." Olasky explained, evidently with the future president's blessing, that "the First Amendment's guarantee of freedom *for* religion should not be taken to mean freedom *from* religion."

Such a blatant distortion of what is at stake in the First Amendment rests on misunderstandings of religion, freedom, and the Constitution.

Freedom is religion's best friend. In reality, authentic personal religion cannot exist apart from an individual's free exercise of will related to beliefs, rituals, confessions, prayers, and institutions. Meaningful personal religion requires that an individual have freedom to make a choice—to believe or not to believe, to pray or not to pray, to join or to remain apart from a religious institution. Young people can be forced to repeat certain words that others call prayers and an adult can be made to voice affirmations of a certain belief, knowing that without that affirmation there will be no wedding, family peace, or vocational success. But a recitation of words must never be confused with prayer or belief. Religion is a matter of the heart. Unless a person is free to reject religion, that person has not experienced the freedom to embrace religion. Freedom always involves choices accompanied by consequences.

At one point in his illustrious career, James Madison saw no need for explicit language assuring religious freedom in the Constitution, believing that such freedom was implicit throughout the document. But he changed his mind. He wrote, "While we assert for ourselves a freedom to embrace, to profess, and to observe the religion which we believe to be of divine origin, we cannot deny an equal freedom to those minds who have not yielded to the evidence which has convinced us. If this freedom be abused, it is an offense against God, not against man: to God, therefore, not to man must an account of it be rendered." Much later, according to a story related by Jon Meacham in *American Gospel: God, the Founding Fathers, and the Making of a Nation*, President Franklin Roosevelt demonstrated his understanding of this principle when he told a friend, "The traditional Jeffersonian principle of religious freedom was so broadly democratic that it included the right to have no religion at all—it gave to the individual the right to worship any God he chose or no god."

The Constitution is concerned with freedom. The free exercise of religion assured in the First Amendment ends at the point at which one person's free exercise impinges on and compromises or eliminates another person's freedom of choice. Framers of the Constitution understood the importance of freedom and never would have allowed a provision called freedom that made no provision for choices. The Constitution provides for people to choose for or against religion.

Myth: America is, and was intended to be, a Christian nation

Some myths do not die easily even if they have been exposed as lies from their inception. The "America is a Christian nation" myth is a case in point.

Demographically, more Americans claim to be Christian than identify with any other religion. In his book *Religious Literacy: What Every American Needs to Know—and Doesn't,* Stephen Prothero observed that, with a Christian population of about 250 million, more Christians live in the United States right now than have ever lived in any other land in the history of the world. But large numbers of people identified with Christianity do not make the nation "Christian." Not only is the claim that America is a Christian nation historically inaccurate, it is also, from one Christian perspective, a theological heresy and likely, when considered carefully by students of American politics, the studied boast of a particular political strategy.

Supporters of the "Christian nation" theory about the United States cherry-pick quotations from various founders of the nation to defend their claim. Most of the founders were far from the kind of avid believers in the Lordship of Jesus Christ and devotion to the Trinitarian God generally associated with Christianity. Additionally, Isaac Kramnick and R. Laurence Moore, in their book *The Godless Constitution: A Moral Defense of the Secular State,* correct the falsehood that all of the colonists were devout, God-fearing people. Some were, no doubt. However, at the time of the Revolution, only 10 to 15 percent of the people belonged to any church. Hector St. John de Crèvocoeur, a French visitor to America and a keen observer in this time described the pervasiveness of religious indifference. Kramnick and Kramer have written, "Americans in 1776 had a long way to go before making themselves strongly Christian or strongly anything else relating to a religious persuasion."

An early legal statement endorsed by the United States government reflected the thought and intent of the founders. In the late 1700s, pirates along the Barbary Coast regularly attacked merchant ships from the colonies that would become the United States. Seeking protection for these vessels and the workers aboard them, the United States government negotiated a treaty with the Kingdom of Tripoli, accompanied by large payments of money and material goods. In exchange, the people of Tripoli were to protect American ships from attacks by pirates. This arrangement was formalized in the Barbary Treaties signed in Tripoli on November 4, 1796, approved by then president of the United States John Adams, and ratified by the United States Senate on June 10, 1797. Article 11 of that treaty, written in Arabic, begins with these words: "As the government of the United States is not in any sense founded on the Christian Religion..." The wording in this historic document was written and affirmed by the very people who had penned the Constitution and the First Amendment. John Adams approved the treaty even though he offered no reproach to people who identified the nation as Christian and called for its leaders to be Christian. Many of the senators who signed the treaty were the founders of the nation, who had included no reference to God in the Constitution. All of the members of the Senate were close enough to the nation's birth to know its founders' thoughts. Clearly, as evidenced in this treaty, they intended no religious identity for the nation.

Most of the claims of a "Christian America" come from Christians. How ironic! Christians sensitive to biblical and theological orthodoxy know that *Christian* is not a word appropriately used as an adjective to describe an institution or an individual with a secular identity. The noun and the adjective negate each other reciprocally. The word *Christian* describes a follower of Christ, an individual in a personal relationship with the Christ. No nation could ever justify the description of "Christian."

Typically, advocates of "America is a Christian nation" voice their view to support the legislation of their sectarian values or the election of candidates for public office whom they deem "chosen and blessed by God." Many starved-for-affirmation politicians readily accept the terminology because it provides them with another campaign strategy—an appeal to faith-based voters and a promise to keep the nation "Christian."

The government of the United States is secular in nature. That is by intent and design. The name of God is not in the United States Constitution; framers of this historic document left out even a reference to the God of Nature referred to in the Declaration of Independence. The omission of the name of a Deity and any mention of religion in the Constitution enraged many people. But the architects of our nation stood firm in their resistance to this criticism. Such has been the story in subsequent years as attempts have been made to amend the Constitution to insert into it the name of Jesus (1947 and 1954) or to make its text more Christian (1864). In fact, the most intense advocates for the secular nature of the United States government have been the people who are most respectful of religion and devoted to preserving its integrity.

Myth: There's a war on Christianity
under way in the United States

This rapidly spreading myth developed only recently. Frankly, the first time I heard it, I laughed. Christians in the United States live the freest, most privileged lives of Christians anywhere in the world. Religion generally enjoys a place of prominence and respect in this nation that is as far from war as peace is from violence. The vitality of Christianity in the United States and the right for evangelicals to engage in aggressive evangelization betray the falsehood involved in the incredible charge of a war against Christianity.

This particular myth got a big boost when Rick Scarborough convened a major conference on "The War on Christians and the Values Voters in 2006" in the spring of that year. In a speech at the conference, former congressman Tom DeLay chided the "chattering classes" who deny a war on Christians. A senior fellow at the Hudson Institute, Michael Horowitz, told the four hundred attendees, "You guys have become the Jews of the twenty-first century" (*Washington Post,* March 29, 2006, A 12) .

Traditionally, many Christians have affirmed the importance of the principle of religious liberty as laid out in the Constitution while taking for granted the unspoken assumption that Christianity really is the established religion in this nation. As I was growing up, people would say, "Look around, quotations from the holy scriptures are chiseled into national monuments, the president of the United States pledges that he will defend the Constitution with his hand resting on a Bible, municipalities hold Christmas festivals and public schools hold Christmas programs, the Supreme Court convenes with a recognition of God, city council meetings open with a prayer from a Christian minister." All of that was true, and some of it still is true. But changes have begun to take place—changes long overdue in a nation dedicated to the vision within its Constitution. While some of us see these changes as an important correction within a religiously pluralistic nation, some Christians, particularly evangelical Christians, consider the enforcement of religious freedom as a war on religion.

The "war" terminology itself drives home the necessity of more stringent compliance with the Constitution. When compliance with the Constitution is considered a war on any religion, something is badly wrong in the nation. However, for many years, many Christians basically ignored the constitutional vision because they were a majority in many regions of the country and behaved as if they belonged to an established church.

This myth of a war on Christianity was born of political ambition and nurtured by thoughtful political strategy. So ludicrous is the imagery peddled by this myth and so out of touch with reality are its claims that I sometimes suspect that the whole outcry about a "war against Christianity" is just more rhetorical hype intended to move more people into the organizational grasp of the Religious Right.

Unfortunately, opportunistic politicians have latched on to this myth with gratitude for yet another electoral strategy. Candidates seem to do well when they play to the galleries of people wanting special privileges for members of the religion in the nation that claims the most adherents.

A reality check always proves helpful. Denial of exceptionalism for Christianity is a far cry from a war on Christianity. If any faith is under attack in this nation, it certainly is not Christianity.

Interestingly, though, without the protection of religious liberty, there would always be a possibility of a war on Christianity or any other religion. One of the great blessings of the First Amendment is that it is a provision of religious freedom that allows all religions to flourish without fear of each other or the government; and it allows all religions the confidence of free expression in the American marketplace of ideas without negative consequences.

CONNECTING DOTS

Any sound strategy for strengthening religious liberty requires connecting dots. Remember the story of my breakfast with the public relations expert. There are untold scores of people just like her. They find the topic of religious freedom rather theoretical and set it aside as not pragmatic enough to merit their thoughts and actions. Only as people recognize the inseparable connection between the political and social issues they care most about and the constitutional provision of religious liberty will they be motivated to pick up that cause with the same intense enthusiasm they give to other causes.

Allow me briefly to connect a few dots.

From Justice Sunday . . . to . . . threats of a "nuclear option" in the United States Senate . . . to . . . regression in minority rights . . . to . . . compromise on religious liberty

Some of us saw it coming. Several Religious Right organizations announced the launch of "Justice Sunday I" in April 2005. Few could argue with the title of such an event other than to point out that every Sunday should be a "Justice Sunday." But, of course, there was more to it than that. Pat Robertson had prayed that God would bring about changes among justices on the United States Supreme Court. Now activists were organizing to pressure United States senators to approve without hesitation President Bush's nominations for federal courts with an eye on ultimately naming a nominee for the Supreme Court. Publicity for "Justice Sunday II," in August of the same year, was built around the cry, "May God save this honorable court," words that are a part of the oral announcement by the Court's marshal as the nine justices of the Supreme Court enter the chamber when the high court is in session. These words were captured for the campaign to suggest that God could only save the court if the Senate confirmed conservative judges who met the criteria of the Religious Right.

Here was the plan. Republicans in the Senate feared that a Democrat who opposed the confirmation of a judicial nominee but recognized that the nominee could not be defeated along a party line vote would choose to launch the time-honored strategy of a filibuster. The filibuster is a tactic of endless speaking so as to prohibit the normal business of the Senate from continuing. In this case, that would mean that no vote could be taken to confirm a judicial nominee. Thus, Republicans in the Senate planned a response to such an effort that was so dramatic and unprecedented that it was labeled "nuclear." The majority leader in the Senate at the time, Republican Bill Frist, who delivered a message to the first "Justice Sunday" gathering, warned that he would not hesitate to employ the "nuclear option." That meant that Senator Frist would take a vote that, given the Republican majority in the Senate, would overrule the right of a senator to use the filibuster as a means of stopping the confirmation vote on a judicial nominee.

When The Interfaith Alliance criticized the threat of eliminating the filibuster, numerous people asked, "Why? By what stretch of the imagination could a filibuster in the United States Senate be considered an issue of importance to people concerned about religious liberty?" At first glance, no connection between eliminating the tactic of the filibuster and protecting religious freedom was obvious. A deeper look, however, heightened awareness of our cause for concern.

Framers of the Constitution entrusted to members of the United States Senate the crucial responsibility of providing for expressions of minority points of view. Every United States senator has the right to filibuster a piece of legislation or a particular judicial nomination that, despite strong and principled opposition by the minority, is likely to be passed by the majority. In debate over a judicial nomination, the filibuster has always stood as a means of promoting accountability and seeking compromise. Thus, removing this unique provision of democracy would upset the founders' carefully developed system of checks and balances that guarantees a full debate in the Senate, and would open the door to a form of tyranny that pays no attention to the minority political party or to dissenters within the majority political party.

Here is the kind of action that has a chilling affect on the nation—discouraging civic participation, eliminating a historic democratic provision at the highest level of government, and setting in place a means of ignoring minority points of view in a manner contradictory to the intention of the nation's founders, many of whom came to this country seeking relief from a tyrannical religious majority in government.

Connect the dots and you see an interest in the Senate's quick confirmation of judicial nominees that tolerates no dissenting points of view or requests for lengthy debates on a nominee's expertise and accountability. Senators in the minority party who honestly questioned whether the experience and vision of a judicial nominee were sufficient for confirmation were harshly charged with attempts to slow down the judicial process. Senators in the majority party laid the groundwork for new Senate rules in which a majority could completely ignore the rights of the minority and function with tyranny. Such a development would alter the nature of democracy and set a precedent for allowing a similar rejection of minority rights in relation to religious liberty.

From concern for Terri Schiavo dying with dignity . . . to
. . . members of the United States Congress and the
President of the United States grandstanding dramatically
. . . to . . . the Religious Right placing freedom under siege . . .
to . . . jeopardizing religious liberty

In 1998, Terri Schiavo's husband petitioned to have her feeding tube removed. Medical experts had declared her brain dead with no hope of recovery; her husband wanted to let her die with dignity. However, Ms. Schiavo's mother and father went to extraordinary efforts to prevent their son-in-law from authorizing the removal of her feeding tubes. With gross insensitivity and a furor aimed at politicizing a family's struggle over how best to demonstrate love for one of its members, Religious Right leaders jumped into the middle of this sad situation to aid their organizational agendas and help build support for their candidates in the upcoming congressional elections.

In March 2005, Republican leaders called members of the Congress to an extraordinary session of that body for the singular purpose of passing a piece of legislation that would require keeping Ms. Schiavo alive. The president of the United States interrupted his vacation to return to Washington in order to sign a hastily written bill that dictated what medical care was to be given to Ms. Schiavo.

Why such urgent attention to one family in a situation that is repeated numerous times every week across the nation? This frenetic flurry of activity was not about what was best, and certainly not about what was most loving, for Terri Schiavo. The business at hand was a political power play to demonstrate that if the government of the United States could move into a terminal care facility in Florida and, by legislative fiat, determine the fate of a brain-dead woman kept alive mechanically, it could win the next election and gain access to the bedrooms, family rooms, and private spaces of people all over the nation.

As members of the Religious Right and officials of the federal government and the state of Florida ripped at the emotions of a grieving husband and the patient's hurting parents, they also sought to tear apart the fabric of religious liberty in this nation. Unlike other cloaked attacks on citizens' basic rights and freedoms that went unrecognized and thus unacknowledged, in this instance the American people immediately connected the dots involved and voiced their outrage. An ABC News Poll on March 20, 2005, indicated that 60 percent of the American people opposed federal intervention in the Schiavo situation. Even 50 percent of evangelical Christians opposed government intrusion into this family situation. In fact, contrary to the hyperbolic rhetoric and frenetic actions of members of Congress and the staff of the White House, 63 percent of the American public supported the removal of the feeding tube from Ms. Schiavo (among evangelical Christians, support for the removal of the tube was at 46 percent with opposition at 44 percent). Freedom-loving people did not want government officials intruding into their families' private conversations and unconscionably meddling in private decisions.

While strategists for the Religious Right's legislative agenda joined forces with conservative political leaders looking for an emotional campaign issue, solid citizens said, "Enough!" Democracy as we have known it was at stake in that life-support-systems-filled room in Florida, where the outlandish intrusion of the government in private decision making and the astounding overreach of government officials were stopped at the door. Thoughtful persons understood that if the government were allowed to push its way into the most private conversations of a family, that government would eventually find a way to define moral values and determine the nature of acceptable religion for everybody.

A call for a balanced science curriculum ... to ... support for freedom of choice in education ... to ... building support for educational vouchers in the form of government finances ... to ... attacks on public schools ... to ... support for indoctrination and proselytism in the name of education ... to ... broadsides against religious liberty

Public schools have become a primary battleground on which religious fundamentalists and political conservatives want to defeat the nation's historic commitment to religious freedom and tear down all walls of institutional separation between religion and government. On this issue, many well-intentioned individuals are tricked by the manipulation of language used to build support for initiatives that are detrimental to liberty. For example, supporters of a science curriculum that teaches a literal seven days of creation or the origins of humankind in a garden called Eden with two people named Adam and Eve brag of their interest in students being exposed to all points of view. Similarly, advocates of public tax dollars being used to support private religious education advance an argument of fairness, declaring that all children should have a right to the best education possible and that children limited to a lack of quality education in public schools should be aided by the government in their search for indoctrination in religious-based private schools.

None of this palaver is about better education. Rather, its interest is a circumvention of religious freedom that will allow schools to teach faith as science, to treat a literal translation of nonhistorical biblical narratives as the laboratory notes of a scientist exploring the origins of life, and to fund efforts at gaining proselytes dedicated to a particular religious point of view under the guise of developing students.

From gay bashing ... to ... programs to "cure" homosexuality ... to ... affirmations of the importance of "traditional" marriage ... to ... advocacy for a proposed federal marriage amendment ... to ... a conclusion that would eviscerate the separation of religion and government, church and state

In this country, various religions with different scriptural traditions embrace diverse views on sexual orientation, scriptural interpretation, and the meaning of marriage. Each has a right to hold its position and to ritualize it within its houses of meditation and worship. That is a matter of religion! At the same time, on this subject as on many others, the institutions of government have no right to establish the views of one religious tradition over another or of religion itself over nonreligion. The government has a constitutional responsibility to treat all religions alike and to guarantee to all people, regardless of their religion, the same rights and privileges afforded to any one.

This situation is devoid of ambiguity. Any benefits the government extends to one citizen should be extended to all citizens. If marriage is a legal contract based on a license purchased from a government entity—and that is the way marriage occurs in this nation—then that government entity must be evenhanded in the extension of its services.

On the other hand, religious institutions have a right to hold different opinions on marriage—who qualifies for marriage, to whom religions will extend their blessings in marriage, and their approval or disapproval of what should be considered "proper" or "moral" marital relationships. And the government has no right to intrude into this process by telling a church, a gurdwara, a mosque, or a temple whom it has permission to declare married and by what ritual.

Again, connect the dots. Condemnations of homosexuality by politicians emerge from campaign strategies aimed at strengthening bases of support. The public rhetoric of denunciation, exceptions, and exclusion promulgated by the leaders of our government points to serious questions about the strength and stability of equal rights. Just as houses of worship do not have a right to impose their views on the sanctity of marriage onto the government or other religious traditions, neither does the government have the right to impose its views on sacred topics onto houses of worship or to seek to make legal for all what is sacred only to some.

What often appears as a moral debate on homosexuality is, in fact, the short fuse on a bomb intended to blow into extinction the First Amendment's clauses guaranteeing religious freedom. The proper conclusion to this discussion, whatever a person's or a religious institution's view on same-sex marriage, is to post a huge sign that says to the government, "KEEP OUT OF OUR HOUSES OF WORSHIP." There is no more fundamental exhortation supportive of religious liberty than that!

From opposition to hate crimes prevention legislation
under the guise of free speech ... to ... diversionary
tactics ... to ... spurious arguments ... to ... insensitivity
to religious liberty

Religious communities in this nation are marked by dramatic differences. Yet these communities consistently speak together, vehemently condemning hate as neither a religious nor a democratic
value. How any compassionate citizen or any religious person could
oppose comprehensive legislation to combat these crimes baffles
the mind, but they do. A few voices arrogantly claiming to be defending freedom and speaking for the majority of Americans regularly seek the defeat of laws against hate crimes. Occasionally, as
happened in an early 2007 congressional debate on hate crimes legislation, these people object to overzealous law enforcement criminalizing thought or speech. The hate crimes legislation will rob us
of free speech, Religious Right lobbyists warned. The rationale
sounds so elevated and sensitive. Don't be fooled. Connect the dots.

The purpose of hate crimes legislation is only to permit federal
prosecution of a hate crime if it is based on the race, color, religion,
national origin, ethnicity, sexual orientation, gender, or disability of
the victim. The law allows the federal government to provide resources to local jurisdictions that may not have the resources to investigate and prosecute these heinous acts.

Some voices from the Religious Right have argued that such legislation would threaten to silence ministers who preach against
homosexuality! But the legislation addresses violent crimes, not
speech. Thankfully, a supermajority of Americans—68 percent,
according to a May 2007 Gallup poll—see through such hyperbolic
arguments and support such legislation, as do law enforcement and
civil rights agencies.

Religious liberty is strengthened, not compromised, by hate
crimes legislation. Religious liberty seeks respect among people
and institutions of religion for those who differ from their point of
view, as well as interest in maintaining a society that appreciatively

embraces pluralism. Opponents of hate crimes legislation are reflecting their religious-based biases, not their concern for a free exercise of religion protected from hate-filled attacks.

From cries of support for free speech ... to ... a circumvention of campaign finance laws ... to ... an affirmation of politicking in houses of worship ... to a weakening of religious liberty

Repeatedly, but as yet unsuccessfully, the Religious Right has attempted to pass a bill (the most recent version of which was called Houses of Worship Free Speech Restoration Act) that would permit houses of worship to endorse candidates for public office from their pulpits, bemas, lecterns, and business desks without losing their tax-exempt status. Look carefully here. This is not about free speech. Ministers in every religious tradition in this nation have a civil right (and I would add a moral responsibility) to interpret social-political issues from the perspective of their respective scriptural traditions. However, to allow a tax-free religious entity to endorse a candidate for public office transforms the house of worship into a political institution. Such a transformation is permissible under the Constitution with this caveat: a religious leader cannot preside over a political organization and receive the IRS benefits of tax exemption.

If enacted, this dangerous piece of legislation would reconfigure the religious landscape of America and deal one of the most damaging blows ever to the First Amendment to the Constitution. Religion would be defined by political loyalty as well as by scriptural beliefs and spiritual practices. Congregations could be divided because of politics and robbed of ministers who stand above political partisanship in their religious ministries.

Connect the dots. IRS regulations impede ministers and other religious leaders from engaging in partisan politics within a house of worship, lest the wall of separation of church and state be breached and the integrity of religion compromised. Make no mistake about it, people supportive of this legislation are not alarmed

at a restriction of freedom nearly so much as they are bothered by
the fact that they cannot set aside the First Amendment to the Constitution.

**From concern for better-funded social services ... to ... a call
for a more compassionate government ... to ... welfare reform ...
to ... government funding for religious ministries ... to ...
an attempt to blast a hole through the First Amendment and
establish government-subsidized religion**

I vividly recall watching a dramatic change on the face of a congressman, as if a bright lightbulb had just come on in his head,
and seeing his mouth literally drop open with the astonishment
engendered by a new insight, when I said that one of my grave concerns with the so-called faith-based initiative is that it compromises the integrity of religion. The setting was a congressional
committee hearing convened to consider whether or not the current White House Office of Faith-Based and Community Initiatives
should be made permanent by legislative mandate. Obviously, I opposed the bill.

Without even considering the questionable political motiva-
tions behind the launch of the faith-based initiative, I have opposed
its existence since the 1999 primary elections in which it was first
nationally discussed. Frankly, opposition to additional money for
religion-oriented social services and even expansion of the buildings and programs of houses of worship has seemed discordant
coming from a Baptist minister. However, the faith-based initiative
is not about faith or social services so much as about political influence, sectarian preferences, and opposition to religious freedom.

Interpretations of the meaning of "make no law respecting an
establishment of religion" have varied widely. However, I know of
no credible First Amendment scholar who would argue the fact
that, from the perspective of "original intent," through the First
Amendment the framers of the Constitution intended to prohibit
any financial support for religion by means of public tax dollars.

Not even the president of the United States or any of the people he has chosen to run the White House Office of Faith-Based and Community Initiatives has been able to explain how the government's financial support for a faith-based initiative will not result in government-subsidized religion.

Many of the well-documented consequences of support for this initiative are telling. Support for the faith based initiative has resulted in the first major attempts to roll back civil rights laws in our nation—and that in the name of support for religion. This initiative effectively makes the religious institutions it funds contractors with and employees of the government agency that provides the money: clearly a violation of church-state separation by any measurement.

In the congressional hearing room in which I made the statement about the faith-based initiative compromising the integrity of religion, I heard prior advocates for the president's priority program confessing that they had not received the money promised or benefited from the financial support of businesses that the president indicated he would enlist. Indeed, an employee of that office, who remains a friend of President Bush, testified in that hearing, and later published in a book, his judgment that the faith-based initiative was a "shell game." As you can read in *Tempting Faith: An Inside Story of Political Seduction*, David Kuo finally had connected the dots.

Truth and consequences

Take any one of the above issues alone and you might conclude that nothing was amiss, that someone shortsightedly launched a campaign without carefully considering its negative impact on religious freedom. But that has not been the case. Taken together, you see that most of the major programs cooperatively launched by the Religious Right with policymakers in the Bush administration have had religious liberty in the crosshairs.

Now, if you will, connect one more set of dots. Move from all of the above—taking all of it together—to the end involved. Immediately you will see three realities that are as common as they are cause for serious concern.

First, all of these issues involve a prioritizing of states' rights over federal rights. That is because many of the supporters of these initiatives consider religious liberty a states' rights issue. If that opinion were affirmed by national legislation and public support, then the resolution of religious liberty conflicts would occur in local communities, local school boards, local zoning commissions, and local human rights boards, guided by the majority religious voice in their respective communities. And, not by coincidence, the Religious Right has done its most extensive organizing in local communities. Who can ever forget this disclosure from the Religious Right's chief strategist Ralph Reed: "I want to be invisible. I do guerilla warfare. I paint my face and travel at night. You don't know it's over until you're in a body bag. You don't know until election night" (*The Hill*, December 17, 1997). Success in relegating religious liberty issues to states' rights issues would devastate our first freedom, on whose foundation all of our other freedoms were constructed.

Second, all of these issues involve an implicit recommendation of a state religion, an established religion. The loudest voices of advocacy for a federal marriage amendment, a faith-based initiative, and vouchers to support private education are the loudest voices of advocacy for sectarian legislation and a vision of government as a tool of religion.

Third, connecting the dots leads one to a frightening conclusion about a master plan for running the nation with an attitude of religious arrogance and no regard for a Constitution that guarantees people freedom from religion as well as freedom for religion.

Perhaps you are aghast. I hope so. Some of you may think me paranoid, laying out evidence of a master plan by which the Religious Right seeks to run the nation. You got it! The Religious Right is responsible for few, if any accidents. The movement works with great deliberation, intention, and focus. It was not by happenstance that both Jerry Falwell and Pat Robertson opened universities distinguished for their excellence in legal education, communication skills, debate, and other training needed to advance the Religious

Right's cause through media, law suits, public relations, community organizing, and hardball politics!

Educating the public about religious freedom is indispensable work. But education must take place alongside civil action. Increasing the public's understanding of religious liberty is best accompanied by efforts to strengthen the vitality of democracy and protect the integrity of religion.

> "Honestly, I'm considering opening up my own church. The way the government is throwing money at them."
> MAN, Cleveland

Strengthening Democracy: Confronting Challenges and Seizing Opportunities

Political action must accompany public education if we are to halt the erosion and shore up the strength of religious liberty. Frankly, the lack of support for religious freedom has reached such crisis proportions that corrections must be made by civil legislation as well as by public education. While attempting to change the minds of Americans who have no sense of the meaning and importance of religious liberty, simultaneous efforts must be under way to counter what is happening in government that is detrimental to the preservation of religious liberty.

No branch of government can be ignored. Since 2001, the executive branch of our government has used the power of executive order to circumvent the resistance of Congress to directing federal funds into religious programs. White House staff members have brought Religious Right leaders into the innermost circles of decision making and sent them out as evangelists of the administration's message regarding "the wonder-working power" of faith-based initiatives. The judicial branch of government has demonstrated an alarming shift toward deference to religious majorities. As newly configured with the addition of Chief Justice Roberts and Associate Justice Alito, the high court seems willing to allow government intrusion into houses of worship, and to give a pass to decisions that, for many, portend tolerance of an official unofficially established religion. (During this same period, though, the United States Senate has prevented a bill authorizing and funding faith-based initiatives, and members of both houses of Congress have enthusiastically fought off attempts to amend social legislation, such as the reauthorization of Head Start, jobs bills, and welfare reform, to give religious institutions money while exempting these organizations from meeting civil rights standards and complying with basic regulatory policies.)

So much of what is weakening religious freedom in the halls of government is not even about religion, and it is certainly not about freedom. The goals driving rhetoric and actions among many governmental leaders primarily involve strengthening political bases and manipulating uninformed public opinion to advance a partisan political agenda.

Again, look carefully at the strategy. When successful in redefining the First Amendment, politicians eager to advance their partisan agendas in the name of religion secure for themselves a broad scope of freedom. Respect for religion can be cited as the fundamental reason for opposing issues like abortion, embryonic stem cell research, and providing civil rights to all citizens regardless of their sexual orientation. It can also be framed as the reason for supporting issues such as teaching faith along with science in public schools and providing vouchers in support of religious indoctrination in private schools.

There are ceaseless attempts to establish through legislation the goals of people who are discontented with the fairness and equality with which the First Amendment treats all religions, as well as venues in which public assaults on religious freedom can be leveled. Such is the not-too-well-hidden strategy behind efforts to change IRS regulations so as to allow religious leaders and houses of worship to make partisan political endorsements without losing their preferred tax-exempt status. Many ambitious politicians have discovered that securing the blessing of megachurch leaders in the Religious Right tradition pays huge dividends in electoral campaigns. Why would they not want the endorsements of houses of worship devoid of penalties for those involved? Not only would the enactment of such legislation harm the political process, but its negative impact on the integrity of religion and religious leaders almost defies comprehension. Yet, as for the issue of religious liberty, they seem to take the position of "who cares?"

Abstinence from political action is no longer an option for people who sincerely care about preserving religious freedom. The hearts and minds of the American public must be changed to favor religious liberty. But while the educational effort proceeds, the votes of legislators and the executive orders of the president must be changed as well.

Exemplary of the challenges to be addressed are two concerns that can best be countered by strategic, grassroots political action.

GOVERNMENT-SUBSIDIZED RELIGION

One of the most vicious broadsides against religious liberty in recent history has been an initiative launched by the White House that has not been approved or funded by Congress; it is perpetuated only by a presidential executive order. Billions of dollars have been funneled into sectarian institutions in direct violation of the Establishment Clause in the First Amendment to the Constitution. Yet so eager are religious people to get their hands on government money to enhance and expand their ministries, so oblivious is the public to the dangers of a loss of religious freedom, and so adept are the political strategies that form the foundation for this program, that the faith-based initiative continues unabated. In reality, the program never has done as much good as the public relations spin would indicate. Nevertheless, the program has persisted with virtually no opposition from the right and only minimal opposition from the left. An astonishingly large segment of the progressive religious community has considered attempts to shut down this initiative much ado about nothing. Indeed, some of the leading voices in the progressive community have been standing with their hands out alongside their conservative counterparts.

Though the official faith-based initiative launched by the White House has never received congressional affirmation, the influence of that program can be seen in piece after piece of legislation. In addition to establishing the Office of Faith-Based and Community Initiatives in the White House, President Bush set up faith-based offices in virtually every agency headed by a member of his cabinet, and he encouraged state governments to take the same action. Subsequently, money has been given to houses of worship to renovate their sanctuaries and expand the space devoted to work in social services.

President Bush has left no doubts about the purpose of his faith-based initiative. During a visit to Louisiana in January 2004, he spoke in the Union Bethel AME Church in New Orleans. I happened to be at my home in Louisiana on the day of this speech, January 16. In fact, I watched local television coverage of President Bush's address with bewilderment and dismay. It was the most explicit statement I have heard him make about the religious purposes behind his allocation of government funding for the faith-based initiative. But the speech received only scant national attention.

Predictably, some of the most disturbing comments about the faith-based initiative came during the president's extemporaneous remarks. After acknowledging that the Union Bethel AME congregation received federal funding for its child care program, the president said, "The handbook of this particular child care is a universal handbook, it's been around a long time." At that point, he turned to Reverend Thomas Brown, the pastor of the congregation, and said, "Let me see your handbook there." The pastor handed his Bible to the president. Holding the Bible up for all to see, President Bush continued his remarks: "This handbook is a good book, it's a good go-by." The official transcript of the president's remark posted on the White House Web site shows that laughter occurred several times during this part of the speech, but the transcript does not preserve the president's off-the-cuff comments. As I watched this televised event, I shuddered to hear the president speak of the Bible as the handbook for the faith-based initiative and explicitly declare that the purpose of the faith-based initiative was changing people's lives—affecting transformation—an experience to which, earlier in his printed remarks, he alluded as "miracles." President Bush told his excited listeners that understanding the faith-based initiative "requires a willingness to understand the origin of miracle." "There is the miracle of salvation in our—." This sentence was not completed, though the official transcript follows the statement with a hyphen, after which another phrase appears: "that is real, that is tangible, that is available for all to see. Miracles are possible in our society, one person at a time." My problem and our nation's problem with this message is that the president was speaking about funding for a church's ministry in a speech identified on the White House Web site as "President Explains Faith-Based Initiative."

When public funds started flowing into the coffers of sectarian organizations, even the White House had to address the issue of the role of civil rights in government-subsidized religion. Though the White House wanted to treat faith-based ministries in the same manner as social services executed by secular organizations, it did not want to compromise the unique identity of houses of worship and other sectarian entities. The solution to the problem took the form of major regression in the support of civil rights guarantees. Working with like-minded members of Congress, the administration developed a strategy to amend all social service legislation with a provision that allowed religious agencies to receive government funds but remain exempt from civil rights laws. Talk about having your cake and eating it, too. Many religious leaders wanted their institutions to be treated with a level of equality provided to secular institutions when it came to the blessings of government funds, but to be treated distinctively, uniquely, when it came to meeting the responsibilities of federally funded organizations and programs.

Since the Bush administration has made the faith-based initiative such a prominent part of public policy discussions, subsequent administrations will have to make decisions about this program. Deciding to ditch it will not be easy for any future administration because of the ability of spin machines to depict opposition to the faith-based initiative as negativity toward religion.

The president who succeeds George W. Bush should end the faith-based initiative and no future president should establish a White House Office of Faith-Based and Community Initiatives. Government has work to do and programs to fund to be true to its responsibility of providing for the public welfare. The nation does not need a government promoting and funding religion. This issue will continue to appear throughout this book as a major challenge threatening the constitutional guarantee of religious freedom.

COURT-STRIPPING BILLS

When viewed from the perspective of religious liberty, a host of congressional proposals are equally repulsive as antics related to faith-based initiatives. Over the past decade, so many congressional deliberations and actions have proven horrendously contradictory to the First Amendment that a plethora of lawsuits has arisen in an effort to stop this vicious assault on the Constitution. Many of these will be discussed later in this book. In reaction to these legal attempts to protect religious freedom, Congress has actually tried to pass legislation to discourage a legal defense of religious freedom.

Bills such as the so-called Public Expression of Religion Act would bar the recovery of attorneys' fees to those who win lawsuits asserting their fundamental constitutional and civil rights in cases brought under the Establishment Clause of the First Amendment. Similarly, Congress has passed a series of "court-stripping" bills (including the Pledge Protection Act) that would prohibit courts from hearing cases on certain subjects that involve church-state questions and relations. In 2004, the House passed the Marriage Protection Act, denying courts the right to rule on the constitutionality of any marriage. This legislation is a blatant assault on our constitutional separation of powers and should be seen as a public alert to theocratic tendencies among people who want their religion to rule our government.

Court-stripping legislation restricts courts from acting on a wide range of issues. The Pledge Protection Act passed in 2004 prohibits courts from ruling on any case questioning the legality of the Pledge of Allegiance or the use of the word "God" in that pledge. Similarly, the Ten Commandments Defense Act of 2003 and the Constitution Restoration Act of 2004 prevent courts from making decisions about the legality of posting the Ten Commandments in public places. Some court-stripping bills even attempt to limit the kinds of cases that can be heard by the United States Supreme Court. Two sinister purposes pervade all of this legislation—to eliminate the balance of power between the three branches of government as guaranteed in the Constitution, and to deny rights to religious minorities and abrogate the promises of the First Amendment. Succinctly stated, these broadsides against the First Amendment compromise the independence, integrity, nature, and work of religion and blunt the vitality of democracy.

You see the strategy. When courts hand down decisions protecting religious liberty, legislators—state and federal—attempt to pass laws restricting the authority of courts to make such decisions supporting the Constitution. Recently, after a court ruled that the Indiana legislature could not offer sectarian prayers in its sessions, a court-stripping bill was introduced to make state legislatures immune from court decisions. Where will it end?

One of the most egregious of the court-stripping bills—an indication of the wave of the future—is the Constitution Restoration Act that has been introduced into the Idaho legislature. This particular bill would deny all courts—including the Supreme Court—any jurisdiction to review cases challenging a government official's acknowledgment of "God as the sovereign source of law, liberty, and government." The act would close the doors of federal courthouses to religious minorities and others who want to ask the courts to protect their religious and free speech rights. This act would punish judges for even reviewing laws that could threaten the integrity of the U.S. Constitution.

All of the court-stripping laws are bad news, and lawmakers will not alter their actions until we voters tell them such actions will not be tolerated.

Election-year opportunities

Election years present unique opportunities for citizens to demonstrate support for religious liberty. Rarely does a candidate run for office without engaging in some discussion of religion, a subject that merits careful consideration and examination. Candidates who raise the issue of religion in their campaigns have a responsibility to explain their views on the role of religion in government. Indeed, citizens should insist on such an explanation.

Article VI of the Constitution forbids the use of any religious test to determine a candidate's worthiness to serve in a public office. However, this constitutional prohibition is unenforceable in individuals' private decision making. Many citizens openly acknowledge suspicion of or opposition to a candidate who does not embrace religion. Reciprocally, many candidates portray their religion as an attractive qualification for their election to public office. During the 2006 senatorial election in Tennessee, the Democratic candidate taped one of his ads in the sanctuary of a church and repeatedly said that Jesus was his campaign manager.

Clarification of the role of religion in electoral campaigns and in government decision making is essential. To facilitate that clarification, prior to the 2000 national elections The Interfaith Alliance recommended five questions for voters to ask candidates seeking public office. These queries, appropriate for candidates at every level of government, were developed against the backdrop of a multireligious nation and with the goal of citizens becoming better informed about how candidates intend to treat religion in the course of their public service. I recommend these important questions to all who are interested in protecting religion from politicization, protecting politics and government from religiofication, and assuring future leaders' support for religious freedom.

The questions speak for themselves:

1. *What role should and do your religious faith and values play in creating public policy?*

2. *What are your views on the constitutional guarantee of the separation of church and state?*

3. *What active steps have you taken and will you continue to take to show respect for the variety of religious beliefs among your constituents?*

4. *Should a political leader's use of religious language reflect the language of his/her religious tradition, or be more broadly inclusive?*

5. *How do you balance the principles of your faith and your pledge to defend the Constitution, particularly when the two come into conflict?*

One of the strongest statements of support for religious freedom and church-state separation ever made came amid a heated political campaign. In 1960, Senator John F. Kennedy was running for president. Many voters, particularly those in the Christian evangelical tradition, feared that because of his membership in the Roman Catholic Church, if Kennedy were elected to the Oval Office, the Holy See in Rome would have an undue influence on American government. A turning point came on September 12, 1960, when Senator Kennedy addressed the Greater Houston Ministerial Association in Houston, Texas, and straightforwardly took on the issue of the role that his personal religion would play in his public service as president of the United States:

> I believe in an America where the separation of church and state is absolute—where no Catholic prelate would tell the President (should he be Catholic) how to act, and no Protestant minister would tell his parishioners for whom to vote—where no church or church school is granted any public funds or political preference—and where no man is denied public office merely because his religion differs from the President who might appoint him or the people who might elect him.

Senator Kennedy's vision of the nation was a contemporary articulation of the vision of the Constitution:

> I believe in an America that is officially neither Catholic, Protestant nor Jewish—where no public official either requests or accepts instructions on public policy from the Pope, the National Council of Churches or any other ecclesiastical source—where no religious body seeks to impose its will directly or indirectly upon the general populace or the public acts of its officials—and where religious liberty is so indivisible that an act against one church is treated as an act against all.

In retrospect, candidate Kennedy's words read today like a challenging, correcting, prophetic oracle:

> Finally, I believe in an America where religious intolerance will someday end—where all men and all churches are treated as equal—where every man has the same right to attend or not attend the church of his choice—where there is no Catholic vote, no anti-Catholic vote, no bloc voting of any kind—and where Catholics, Protestants, and Jews, at both the lay and pastoral level, will refrain from those attitudes of disdain and division which have so often marred their works in the past, and promote instead the American ideal of brotherhood.

In his stunning example of helpful campaign rhetoric, John F. Kennedy also modeled the manner in which a public official should view and remain true to his or her personal religious convictions while in public office. "I am not the Catholic candidate for President," Kennedy announced, "I am the Democratic Party's candidate for President who happens also to be a Catholic. I do not speak for my church on public matters—and the church does not speak for me. Whatever issue may come before me as President—on birth control, divorce, censorship, gambling or any other subject—I will make my decision in accordance with these views, in accordance with what my conscience tells me to be the national interest, and without regard to outside religious pressures or dictates. And no power or threat of punishment could cause me to decide otherwise."

Perhaps the most important words Kennedy spoke in Houston were those that demonstrated how much his personal religion meant to him and how important he believed the presidency to be for the nation. Kennedy concluded, "But if the time should ever come—and I do not concede any conflict to be even remotely possible—when my office would require me to either violate my conscience or violate the national interest, then I would resign the office; and I hope any conscientious public servant would do the same."

Every candidate who runs for office in the United States should be able to pledge to American voters no less than Senator Kennedy promised. Every voter has the right to know every candidate's beliefs about the relationship between personal religion (if there is one) and public service under the guidance of the Constitution.

> *"The religion I see being taught today is for the most part a divisive system of indoctrination, even among similar sects. And the extent to which it is being used to control the minds of the masses nowadays for political purposes is disgusting."*
> DORIAN

Protecting Religion:
Integrity and Responsibility

As I mentioned earlier, several months ago I served on a panel convened for a congressional hearing to consider whether or not to assure perpetuation of President George W. Bush's vision of faith-based initiatives. Two pieces of legislation had been proposed to make permanent the White House Office of Faith-Based and Community Initiatives, assuring its existence in succeeding administrations. My response to those proposals was a resounding "no" —no to the proposed legislation and no to the perpetuation of the office.

Just before I spoke to members of Congress, Rabbi David Saperstein had eloquently articulated that a negative response to the proposals was necessary to protect the United States Constitution. I affirmed my support for Rabbi Saperstein's remarks before opposing the proposed legislation for a different reason. I said to committee chairman Mark Souder (R-IN), a compassionate man who strongly supports more assistance for the poorest, weakest, and most needy among us,

> My opposition to this program resides in a profound concern that the program, as presently configured, ultimately will hurt, not help, both the religious community and the civil community in their efforts to meet those needs and possibly impact adversely the people in need as well. . . . I have many constitutional concerns about this program . . . But I speak to you today primarily focused not on what this program does to the Constitution

of our nation but what it does to the vitality and integrity of religion in our nation ... The institutions of government need to stay out of the institutions of religion for the sake of religion.

(Incidentally, my remarks here were not unlike those conveyed earlier in a letter to the Senate opposing the Charity Aid, Recovery, and Empowerment Acts of 2002.)

Lest anyone assume that an interest in protecting the integrity of religion is a selfish cause embraced among religious isolationists, please be aware that protecting the integrity of religion is an integral component in efforts to protect the vitality of democracy. I have no interest in seeking special privilege for religion, only in prohibiting such an entanglement of the institutions of religion and the institutions of government that the integrity of religion is compromised and the vitality of democracy blunted.

Here is a strategy for protecting the integrity of religion amid an environment in which a profusion of religious rhetoric and prolific boasts about the importance of religion provide cover for actions aimed at weakening the promise of religious freedom in the Constitution.

ENCOURAGING RELIGIONS TO ACT LIKE RELIGIONS

Religions make their best contribution to the nation when they behave as religions. Presently, though, government and politicians seem to be pressing hard to move religions in another direction— doing faith-based social work in conjunction with the government providing money to support this activity, and functioning as political action groups to aid "faith-blessed" politicians seeking election to public office. A preoccupation with finding money to expand social services and a passion for politics that serve sectarian interests are propelling religious leaders into a mind-set devoid of sensitivity to the complexities inherent in relationships between pervasively sectarian organizations and governmental agencies and personnel. Subsequently, and ironically, under the guise of advancing religion, religious leaders are threatening the existence of religious freedom

—the constitutional provision that has contributed inestimably to the strength, vibrancy, and pluralism that characterize religion in the nation.

A sure sign of the undue influence of government and politics on religion is the rancorous divisiveness that has fragmented religious communities around the country. In a country that is deeply divided and in need of the positive and healing role that religion can play in a society, religion itself is divided. Moreover, it is divided along precisely the same fault lines that mark political and economic divisions. Religious leaders are incapable of doing work that is essential to religion because they have given themselves to work that is quintessentially political.

Religious leaders have not been passive pawns or resistant victims in what is happening. Leaders in religious organizations have been as eager to use government for sectarian purposes as leaders in government have been to use religious leaders for their partisan purposes. In other words, not all of the problems related to religious liberty reside in government. Unfortunately, religious leaders awed by political power appear to possess no long-range vision of the manner in which they are compromising the integrity of religion, as well as their credibility as religious leaders. Accompanying these consequences, of course, are the first symptoms of a weakened democracy.

When religions try to function as something other than religions, they typically lose their integrity and jeopardize their importance. Religion is neither a puppet of the government nor a puppeteer seeking to pull the strings that control the actions of government leaders. Religion is not a political action group or a bloc of voters like trade unions, farmers, or partisan entities. It is a presence that works for unity, advocates for values such as justice, compassion, and peace, and welcomes into its midst people of all races and socioeconomic status—and even partisan politicians.

Do religious leaders really want government doing the work of religion? Unchecked, such an inclination will inexorably lead to government leaders defining the nature of God (e.g., the patriotic God in the Pledge of Allegiance), legislators prescribing spiritual practices (establishing a civil definition of marriage that must be respected by houses of worship), and the judiciary enforcing postings of scriptures that give prominence to one religious tradition over another. "Think what you are doing!" I want to scream (and sometimes do) at religious leaders inviting government to help do their work. Ultimately, both religion and government will be hurt, badly hurt, by such an arrangement.

REJECTING DESACRALIZATION OF RELIGION

When religious leaders become powerful players in partisan politics, when religious institutions become government-funded institutions, and when religious language becomes the common rhetoric of a society, religion—its institutions, ministries, and language—is compromised, if not de-sacralized.

Whatever one's perspective on whether or not the name of God belongs in the Pledge of Allegiance, everyone would have to admit that the holiness of God took a horrible blow in the discussion of this subject. I recall so well a CNN-televised discussion prompted by the Ninth Circuit Court's decision about the unconstitutionality of using the name of God in the pledge. The network's chief legal analyst observed that the word "God" in the pledge had little religious meaning; it is more of a "patriotic term" than a spiritual term, the man observed. What? When the name that some religious people will not even speak aloud because of its sacredness is considered a term of patriotism with little religious meaning, something is wrong.

A similar desacralization occurs in many discussions about the civil use of the Ten Commandments. Eager to win a political victory by securing the right to post the Ten Commandments in public places, proponents of the posting argue that the commandments should be displayed because of their importance as a legal document. Is that progress for religion—to turn holy scripture into a document with significance because of its contribution to civil law?

Ironically, many of the most avid proponents of using public venues to promote religion fail to recognize that they are hurting religion more than helping it. A national religion—a civil religion that blends special religious language with general national observances, treats historical holy days filled with spiritual significance as government-declared holidays for fun, rest, and relaxation, and develops an iconography of the nation that blends into and rivals in importance the rites and rituals of specific religious traditions—is distinct from the sacred traditions of people who cherish religion as sacred and holy, and as mystery.

HALTING THE ATTACK ON RELIGIOUS FREEDOM

Religious leaders should be the first to step forward in defense of religious liberty. Without this constitutional guarantee, religion in this nation could fall into the same kind of subjugation to government that has happened in so many places around the world. At that point, religion is hurt as much as government.

Religion is a prime beneficiary of religious freedom. In any situation in which people are not free to make personal decisions about religion and to live out the consequences of those decisions, religion is in trouble. Religion can never be imposed. Prayers, meditations, and all forms of worship come from the heart, and none can be prescribed. A repetition of dictated words can sound religious, but if the words do not arise in the heart and find expression because of personal will, they have little, if anything, to do with religion.

Any time a religious leader or a politician criticizes religious freedom, watch out. The person is pursuing an agenda that is more about control than freedom, more about the imposition of a preference than the guarantee of a decision, more about an establishment of religion than the free exercise of religion.

PROMOTING RELIGIOUS PLURALISM

In her excellent book *A New Religious America*, Diana Eck makes an important distinction between religious diversity and religious pluralism. Religious diversity is a fact in the United States. But religious pluralism stems from citizens affirming religious diversity and promoting interreligious cooperation, rather than condemning religious diversity and practicing exclusion, or tolerating religious diversity and working to eliminate it by means of assimilation. Religious pluralism in the United States remains a goal.

Working for religious pluralism involves relentless support for religious freedom. Diverse religions experience a sense of welcome and security, with the promise of partnerships and cooperation, when every religion in the nation enjoys the same benefits as every other religion. Religious pluralism signals the success of religious liberty and of democracy, both of which nurture inclusivity in the nation.

SHORING UP THE "WALL OF SEPARATION"

"Enough already!" is a proper response to the peddlers of lies who seek to distort the blessing of religious freedom by turning it into a curse aimed at doing harm to religion. We need some evangelists for the cause.

If you don't know what to say, turn to Frequently Asked Questions on page 175.

Yes, we need a wall of separation between houses of worship and agencies of government. The religions of the nation must be free from government control—free to worship a deity not defined by the government, to gather in houses of worship not funded by the government, and to engage in ministries not regulated by the government. And the government must be free from the control of religion—legislating sectarian values, devoting the bully pulpit to advance doctrinal affirmations, and converting provision for the public's welfare into initiatives embracing a particular faith. Legal, institutional separation between religion and government is the only way in which beneficial institutional cooperation between religion and government can occur.

Frankly, in a religiously diverse society, the guarantee of religious liberty serves as a prophylactic against war. America has been spared the bloody conflicts between religions that have devastated some parts of the world. Study those situations and you will find that a lack of religious liberty coincides with an abundance of interreligious conflict.

The wall of separation between religion and government benefits both. Church-state separation provides a firm foundation on which religion and government can cooperate with each other without either trying to act as the other or control the other. Securing that relationship moves this nation toward an even greater realization of the vision for it embedded in the Constitution.

Decision Time: A U-turn
or Full Speed Straight Ahead

The erosion of support for our "first freedom" must be halted and cooperation to alter present trends facilitated. Otherwise, the nation will make a U-turn and place itself once again in a pre–First Amendment situation. The dangers involved in that scenario today are qualitatively and quantitatively more significant than they were when the First Amendment was written.

So much is at stake in what happens—the status of religious liberty to be sure, but much, much more. Since religious liberty—our first freedom—serves as the foundation on which other freedoms have been constructed, the demise of this historic guarantee of liberty would weaken, if not destroy, the guarantee of other freedoms and rights as well.

Keep in mind that it was not by accident that the First Amendment to the Constitution included the first freedom—religious freedom. In a flourish of visionary wisdom, the Founding Fathers laid the groundwork for a freedom that was so integral to the country's vision and development that this freedom could be lost only if the nation itself were lost. The reverse was also true: to lose this freedom would be to lose the nation.

At our country's birth, religious freedom, like democracy, was a bold experiment. In reality, it remains an experiment to this day. Religious freedom is not yet secure. It is likely that it will always be under threat. All people, the great Thomas Jefferson included, see more wisely than they act, promise more hopefully than they deliver. A vision can fade. In difficult times of crisis, even freedom can seem expendable and security be viewed as more desirable. Whether the First Amendment to the Constitution could be adopted by a popular vote today remains a serious question.

Our nation has come to a point in its pilgrimage of democratic development where some involved want to make a U-turn and go back to pre–First Amendment days. Those who want to stay the course long for a reinvigoration of our commitment to religious liberty with the intent of moving full speed ahead. We citizens will have to fight to keep the degree of religious liberty that we have enjoyed up to now. We will have to be aggressive in education and action to strengthen religious liberty in a manner that makes it more secure for the future.

Not long ago, while in Boston, I walked again the Freedom Trail that winds its way through that historic city. At the Old South Meeting House, I was deeply moved to find a copy of the religious liberty clauses of the Constitution placed on the communion table. That emotion of appreciation intensified as I was reminded of how the members of that congregation, indeed the whole community, were catapulted into social activism because of their passion for freedom. They were not looking for government funding or undue political influence for institutional benefits. Rather, they were declaring an intention to live in freedom and pledging themselves to fight for the realization of that intent.

Suddenly, I found myself wanting to take the hands of leaders in the upper echelons of our government and some of the more vocal critics of religious liberty in the religious community and ask all of them to walk with me along that Freedom Trail. We would make our way to that old meetinghouse where a commitment to religious freedom is so palpable that all who go there can see and feel it and understand the importance of it. I would point to a plaque that hangs on the lower east gallery level, which is on the left-hand side of the meetinghouse if looking out from the pulpit. The words on that plaque come from an observation made by General George Washington, born of his resentment of the British who had used that sacred space as a venue for training horses. The man who later became our first president said that he found it "strange that the

British who so venerated their own churches, should have thus desecrated ours." Standing in that early place of worship, I would plead with my contemporaries to realize that while they praise the importance of houses of worship in their speeches and sermons they are also compromising, if not desecrating, houses of worship when they attempt to use holy space for their government programs, partisan politicking, and even electoral campaigning. Perhaps the leaders of both religious and governmental communities would rediscover the necessity of keeping separate the institutions of religion and government, thus preserving religious freedom.

Of course, a freedom trail of sorts runs through all of our communities. The future of the lofty principle of religious freedom will be determined by thousands of incidental and intentional decisions that people like you and me make, as well as by legislation Congress enacts, executive orders the president issues, and decisions that the United States Supreme Court and its national family of lower courts hand down.

However, this much is sure: in the final analysis, *we* are the government! Religious freedom will disappear only if we the people, the citizens, allow that tragedy to occur. That must not happen. Religious freedom must be preserved not only for the good of religion but for justice to be done and for the vitality of democracy to be enhanced as well as preserved. What happens next is a matter of will. Religious freedom will continue as a friend to religious and nonreligious citizens alike and as a pivotal contributor to the strength of our democracy, as long as citizens of this nation will that it continue and express that will through public advocacy and political action. So may it be!

Part II: A Legal Perspective

BARRY W. LYNN

A Brief History of
Constitutional Law on Religion

If you listen to the Religious Right's refrain, you might think that religion generally, and Christianity specifically, faces some grave danger in the United States today. The movement's leaders rebuke "unelected black-robed" federal judges for "kicking God out" of our public schools and, indeed, public life. American Christians, they say, are "persecuted" in their own country. It would be alarming if it were true, but it's not.

In fact, the very federal court system that these leaders blame for being "hostile" toward religion has *preserved* the private citizen's ability to publicly express his or her beliefs. Public school students pray in groups and alone every day. It's all quite legal, even sanctioned by the United States Supreme Court. As a minister and civil libertarian, I wouldn't have it any other way. The Supreme Court has also protected every citizen's right to share his or her beliefs, religious or otherwise, in the public square. I applaud their right to do so and would note that there are few people, at least where I work in Washington, DC, who don't take advantage of this right.

The First Amendment protects five distinct freedoms: freedom of religion, freedom of speech, freedom of the press, and the freedoms to peacefully assemble and petition the government. First on the list of the Amendment's enumerated rights is religious freedom: a spare sixteen words that guarantee freedom from state-imposed religion and its costs (the Establishment Clause) and the right to freely exercise one's chosen faith (the Free Exercise Clause). Because religious freedom is the first enumerated right in the Constitution's First Amendment, it is often referred to as America's "first freedom."

It's difficult to know precisely what the first congressmen and state legislators wanted the religion clauses to accomplish. There is no comprehensive record of floor debates, so we depend largely on members' notes and recollections. This makes it exceedingly difficult to determine the founders' "original intent," what so many on the Religious Right say we should use as our sole guide for interpreting the First Amendment.

This does not mean, however, that we lack insight into how or why the founders crafted the religion clauses. We know, for example, that the First Congress considered no fewer than six drafts of the current Establishment and Free Exercise clauses before sending the Bill of Rights to the states for ratification. The Senate and House of Representatives rejected proposals that would have prohibited official "articles of faith or a mode of worship," or the establishment of "any particular denomination of religion in preference to another" (Douglas Laycock, "'Nonpreferential' Aid to Religion, a False Claim about Original Intent." *William and Mary Law Review,* Vol. 27, 1986). This strongly suggests that our founders intended to restrict more than just the establishment of a national church. Instead, the language was deliberately left expansive in scope so future generations could interpret its meaning as it applied to the world they were living in. We also know that President Thomas Jefferson, one of religious liberty's staunchest supporters, thought the religion clauses should separate church and state. He wrote in an 1802 letter to the Danbury Baptists, "that act of the whole American people which declared that their legislature should 'make no law respecting an establishment of religion, or prohibiting the free exercise thereof,' [built] a wall of separation between Church and State."

The religion clauses applied strictly to the federal government until the ratification of the Fourteenth Amendment in 1868 laid the groundwork for holding states to the same standard. One of the Amendment's primary purposes was to eliminate vestiges of slavery, but just as importantly, it protects citizens' federal rights and liberties from state encroachment. The Amendment reads, in part:

"No State shall make or enforce any law which shall abridge the privileges or immunities of citizens of the United States; nor shall any State deprive any person of life, liberty, or property, without due process of law; nor deny to any person within its jurisdiction the equal protection of the laws."

Senator Jacob Howard (R-MI), the Amendment's primary advocate on the Senate floor, said the Amendment's purpose was to rescind any distinction between state and federal governments' power to control their citizens. "To these privileges and immunities," he noted in his speech introducing the Amendment, "should be added the personal rights guaranteed and secured by the first eight amendments to the Constitution.... The great object of the first section of the amendment is therefore to restrain the powers of the state and to compel them at all times to respect these fundamental guarantees." Despite Howard's intention that the first eight amendments be incorporated wholesale, the U.S. Supreme Court waited for individual cases contesting state actions that violated freedoms in those amendments to gradually clarify that the Bill of Rights protected such freedoms from all government transgression.

RELIGIOUS FREEDOM AND THE COURTS: THE EARLY CASES

Few Americans thought of trying religious liberty cases in court prior to the mid-twentieth century. The creation of advocacy groups like Americans United for Separation of Church and State and the American Civil Liberties Union, which educated Americans about their rights, gave many religious minorities the resources and support to challenge federal, state, and local actions.

Only two significant religion cases reached the U.S. Supreme Court before 1940. The first, *Reynolds v. United States,* challenged the federal government's condition that the Utah Territory ban polygamy before it could enter the Union. Although many Utahans were members of the Church of Jesus Christ of Latter-day Saints (also known as Mormons), which claimed plural marriage was a required religious exercise, the Supreme Court decided in 1879 that the U.S.

could indeed ban the practice. The Court unanimously concluded that the federal government could prohibit behavior, even if practitioners claimed it was religiously mandated, that threatened society's stability or well-being. The second, *Pierce v. Society of Sisters*, questioned the constitutionality of Oregon's mandatory public education law. Plaintiffs argued that forcing parents to send their children to common schools (which propagated a generic form of Protestantism at the time) violated their right to direct their children's educational upbringing. The Court agreed, and in 1925 upheld the state's power to compel school attendance, but concluded that religious groups could establish private schools and parents could send their children to either private or public institutions. *Pierce* was actually decided on Fourteenth Amendment grounds, but had the practical effect of significantly furthering free exercise by allowing parents to incorporate their preferred religious teachings into their child's secular education.

I mentioned earlier that the Fourteenth Amendment did not apply the Constitution's first eight amendments to the states wholesale in 1868, but that the U.S. Supreme Court obliged states to protect individual rights and liberties as the opportunities arose through litigation. The Free Exercise Clause was applied to the states in the 1940 case *Cantwell v. Connecticut*. The Establishment Clause followed seven years later in *Everson v. Board of Education*.

Cantwell v. Connecticut involved the right of a Jehovah's Witness to proselytize on a public street. Newton Cantwell and his two sons, Jesse and Russell, wanted to spread their faith in a predominately Roman Catholic neighborhood in New Haven, Connecticut. They went door to door distributing literature and playing records denouncing Catholicism. This didn't sit well with local officials, who arrested, tried, and convicted the Cantwells for soliciting without a permit. They appealed their convictions all the way to the U.S. Supreme Court, and prevailed with a unanimous decision rebuking the state's attempt to curtail their free speech and religious exercise rights. Justice Owen Roberts wrote that the states did not have that power because "The fundamental concept of liberty embodied in the [Fourteenth] Amendment embraces the liberties guaranteed by the First Amendment. The First Amendment declares that Congress shall make no law respecting an establishment of religion or prohibiting the free exercise thereof. The Fourteenth Amendment has rendered the legislatures of the states as incompetent as Congress to enact such [restrictive] laws."

Everson v. Board of Education is a peculiar case. The five-justice majority's decision was not a win for church-state separationists, but the message backed by the entire Court was a ringing endorsement for a solid "wall" between church and state. In 1947, a group of New Jersey taxpayers challenged a state law allowing municipalities to finance private school students' transportation to and from school. Ewing Township had appropriated $357 to bus children to local parochial schools. The taxpayers argued that if the state could not restrict private promotion of religion, as the Court ruled in *Cantwell,* it surely could not promote religion by supporting sectarian schools. The Court agreed—but only in part.

All nine justices supported Justice Hugo Black's assertion that "Neither a state nor the federal government can set up a church... Neither can pass laws which aid one religion, aid all religions, or prefer one religion over another... No person can be punished for entertaining or professing religious beliefs or disbeliefs. No tax in any amount, large or small, can be levied to support any religious activities or institutions, whatever they may be called or whatever form they may adopt to teach or practice religion." Despite Black's seemingly unambiguous guidelines, he was able to convince four colleagues that Ewing's appropriation did *not* constitute religious establishment. The five-justice majority concluded that the expenditure was constitutional for two reasons: first, the schoolchildren's benefit in getting safely to and from school outweighed the taxpayers' burden; and second, the cost of providing that transportation was not sufficient to actually "support" the religious institution. Contradictory rhetoric and rulings not withstanding, *Everson* remains the foundation of church-state separation case law because it forbids state and local governments from actions "respecting an establishment of religion."

For over sixty years, the Court has used *Everson* to uphold some types of public aid to religious institutions, but also to strike down others. A controlling consideration is whether the aid can be used for sectarian purposes. Textbooks and supplies identical to those given to public schools cannot be used for religious ends, the Court determined in a line of cases, but tuition reimbursements for families with children in parochial schools can, and therefore violate the Establishment Clause. Deference paid to that bright line shifted in the 1990s; the Court began to find exceptions to the rule, allowing taxpayer-financed in-kind assistance that could, and indeed was, used for sectarian purposes. In *Zobrest v. Catalina Foothills School District,* for example, the Court concluded that providing a state-employed American Sign Language interpreter for a child attending parochial school did not violate the Establishment Clause. The state of California had argued that providing such a service would facilitate the child's religious education, and therefore violate the Constitution's ban on government actions advancing religion. The Court disagreed, concluding that the state cannot deny adaptive services simply because the recipient is religious.

THE POWER OF PRAYER

Of all of the Supreme Court cases pertaining to religion, perhaps none have been more misunderstood than those dealing with prayer in public schools. We often hear stories of children being punished for praying, reading the Bible, or talking about religion in public schools, but these are nearly always urban legends, or at best, a misrepresentation of the facts.

The Supreme Court's first school prayer case came in 1962's *Engel v. Vitale.* The Court struck down a New York state law which "allowed" public school students at the beginning of each day to voluntarily recite a non-denominational prayer written by a state school commission. Justice Hugo Black wrote for the 7–1 majority, "Neither the fact that the prayer may be denominationally neutral nor the fact that its observance on the part of the students is voluntary can serve to free it from the limitations of the Establishment Clause." Black chided New York education officials for establishing a relationship with religion that resembled the one the first American colonists fled in Europe. Importantly, the Court never ruled that students could not pray on their own. It was the government's decision to write a prayer that was rebuked, not a student's right to speak one.

The following year the Supreme Court considered a similar pair of cases involving devotional Bible reading in Pennsylvania and Maryland public schools. The parallel facts in *Madalyn Murray (O'Hair) v. Curlett* and *Abington School District v. Schempp* were folded together and decided in one case filed under the latter title. Before Edward Schempp's case reached the nation's highest court, each school day in Abington Township, Pennsylvania, began with teachers reading "at least ten verses of the Holy Bible" and leading their classes in the Lord's Prayer. School officials at atheist Madalyn Murray O'Hair's son's public school in Baltimore, Maryland, also led students in Bible reading and the Lord's Prayer each morning. Both laws allowed children to remove themselves to the hallway if they or their parents objected to the collective prayer.

Allowing students to excuse themselves from the exercises was a wholly inadequate response, the Court concluded, for instituting what amounted to an established religion in public schools. Justice Tom C. Clark evoked *Engel* in his 8–1 decision for the Court. "[I]n further elaboration," he wrote, the Court last term "found that the 'first and most immediate purpose [of the Establishment Clause] rested on the belief that a union of government and religion tends to destroy government and degrade religion.'" In other words, when the justices ruled in *Engel* that the First Amendment prohibited the government's imposition of religion and protected the individual's right to practice religion, they did so as much in the interest of religion as they did in the interest of the secular state. Again, the majority in *Abington* did not prohibit a student from saying grace before eating her lunch, or bowing his head before picking up his pencil to take a test. It only restricted the state from determining the time, place, manner, or nature of religious worship.

The Religious Right has clung desperately to *Engel* and *Abington* as "evidence" that God has been "kicked out" of our public schools.

As we'll discover later in this section, their concern may not be about public school students' ability to express their religion as much as it is about the school's power to impose (the Religious Right's narrow interpretation of their particular) religion on students.

In 1971, the Supreme Court handed down a case that connected principles recognized in earlier religious funding and expression cases. In *Lemon* v. *Kurtzman,* the Court invalidated two state laws subsidizing religious schools. Chief Justice Warren Burger established what has become known as the *Lemon* Test in his opinion for the unanimous Court. A law or government action must meet three criteria in order to be considered constitutional under *Lemon.* Failing even one part of the test will invalidate the contested law or action. First, the law or action must have a secular legislative purpose. Second, its principal or primary effect must neither advance nor inhibit religion. Finally, it must not foster excessive "entanglement" between government and religion.

The Religious Right had gained a major foothold in American politics by the time the next public school prayer case reached the Supreme Court. Movement leaders used their newfound power to urge local lawmakers to pass statutes mandating that public school days start with a moment of silence. The Religious Right and its allies in state and local governments saw the laws as a way to circumvent proscriptions on teacher-led prayers in their public schools. The Supreme Court considered such a law passed by Alabama in the 1985 case, *Wallace v. Jaffree.* The new law, which replaced an existing policy allowing for a moment of silence at the beginning of the school day, called for a moment of "silent meditation or voluntary prayer." After reviewing the statute's legislative history, the Supreme Court determined that the law was really only intended to get organized prayer back into the classroom, a fact its supporters readily admitted during legislative debates. Having no secular legislative purpose, the law fell to *Lemon's* first requirement.

Before another decade passed, the Supreme Court would issue its first ruling on whether prayers could be offered at official public school gatherings, such as commencement ceremonies. In *Lee v.*

Weisman, a closely divided Court sided with a Jewish parent from Providence, Rhode Island, who objected to a clergy-led prayer to be given at his daughter's upcoming graduation. Deborah Wiseman's family knew that a clergyman would be invited to give the invocation and benediction at her 1989 middle school graduation. Her father pleaded with a federal court to stop the school's principal from including the prayers, but his attempts were denied, and the principal was allowed to invite a local rabbi to the ceremony. Deborah and her family attended her graduation, forced to acquiesce to the religious practice.

The Supreme Court rebuked the school district for inviting religious leaders to participate in public school ceremonies, reminding officials around the country that the Establishment Clause forbade school stamps of approval on religious activities. Justice Anthony Kennedy did not base the majority opinion on the *Lemon* test, but on the more rigid "coercion test." The "coercion test" asks, as its title implies, if a government law or action compels religious activity or support. Justice Kennedy noted that the Court had often used a "coercion test" when assessing state-sponsored religious activity in public schools because children and teenagers are more susceptible to coercive pressure than adults. The majority opinion concluded that the clergy-led prayers at public school graduations violated the "coercion test" because the "school district's supervision and control of a (public) high school graduation ceremony places public pressure, as well as peer pressure, on attending students" to participate in the prayer or, at the very least, respectfully stand in silence. The fact that students are not compelled to attend graduation in order to receive their diploma, as the state pointed out, was of no comfort to Justice Kennedy. Asking young adults to choose between following their religious beliefs and attending their high school graduation is a false and unacceptable choice, he said.

Lee v. Weisman curbed religious exercises overtly orchestrated by public school officials, but it did not stop them from trying other gimmicks to sneak religion into public school events. In 1995, a Texas school district devised a scheme to let high school students vote on whether to open sporting events (football games, in this case) with a prayer and then to elect a student "chaplain" to lead the prayers. A federal district court upheld the design on the condition that the prayers, to be read over the school's stadium public address system, were "nonsectarian" and "nonproselytizing." The U.S. Fifth Circuit Court of Appeals reversed, and the U.S. Supreme Court upheld, that decision 6–3 in the 2000 case *Santa Fe Independent School District v. Doe*.

Justice John Paul Stevens's majority opinion was both poignant and unforgiving. He drew on sentiment the Court had expressed nearly sixty years earlier. "The very purpose of a Bill of Rights," the prior Court had written, "was to withdraw certain subjects from the vicissitudes of political controversy, to place them beyond the reach of majorities and officials and to establish them as legal principles to be applied by the courts. One's right to life, liberty, and property, to free speech, a free press, freedom of worship and assembly, and other fundamental rights may not be submitted to vote; they depend on the outcome of no elections."

Justice Stevens also said the school district's attempt to spin the prayers as student, not school, speech was unpersuasive. "The delivery of a message such as the invocation here—on school property, at school-sponsored events, over the school's public address system, by a speaker representing the student body, under the supervision of school faculty, and pursuant to a school policy that explicitly and implicitly encourages public prayer—is not properly characterized as 'private' speech." Courts are still assessing the circumstances under which a student speaker can refer to religious beliefs at school-sponsored events. At graduations, the trend is towards allowing students to refer to the role a deity has played in their lives, but not to urge the compliance or conversion of audience members by turning the address into a sermonette. Although critics of this approach assert that such distinctions are difficult to draw, the essence of our legal system is based on drawing lines around what is and is not publicly permissible under our Constitution.

ETCHED IN STONE?

The place of the Ten Commandments and other sacred images and icons in the public square has long symbolized the underlying tension between the right to religious expression and the need for church-state separation. Supporters of their public display say the Commandments are Western law's foundation and remind citizens of their societal duties not to kill, steal, or lie. Supporters of church-state separation correctly argue that the Decalogue is religious law, central to only three of the many faiths practiced in America. Some of the Commandments may parallel secular laws, but their placement in government buildings like public schools and courthouses serves no other purpose than to promote religion.

The first Supreme Court case to challenge the Decalogue's public display was *Stone v. Graham*. The state of Kentucky passed a law in 1978 mandating that all public school classrooms display a copy of the Ten Commandments. The Court struck down the statute in 1980, finding that it failed *Lemon*'s "secular purpose" test. Although these displays were procured by private donations, not taxpayer funds, the Court found that it was inappropriate for public schools to promote a religious text (a text, coincidently, which is translated and interpreted in many different ways).

Another twenty-five years elapsed before the Court took up its next case testing the constitutionality of government displays of the Ten Commandments. Yes, the "wheels of justice" do turn slowly. The core issue in each of the two cases, both argued on March 2, 2005, was the same, but particular fact patterns in each case led a closely divided Court to rule in favor of the Commandments' public display in one case and against their display in the other.

Van Orden v. Perry considered the constitutionality of a six-foot-tall granite monument on the Texas state capitol grounds. The monument had been donated by the Fraternal Order of the Eagles in 1961, and had remained uncontested for forty years. The capitol compound also displayed a number of other religious, historic, and civic monuments. The Court's five-member majority concluded that this diverse collection would not lead viewers to believe that the state of Texas necessarily endorsed the Commandments as a religious text, but rather, at most, recognized their role in Texas law and history. Justice Stephen Breyer wrote in his concurring opinion that the Establishment Clause's underlying purpose was to prevent religious divisiveness in the burgeoning nation. The fact that the monument went uncontested for "nearly two generations" strongly suggested that it had not contributed to any religious tension. In his opinion, this made the Texas monument definitively different from the displays he switched sides to strike down in *Van Orden's* companion case, *McCreary County v. ACLU of Kentucky*.

The displays at issue in *McCreary County v. ACLU of Kentucky* had a much more complex history. In the summer of 1999, the Kentucky state legislature passed a resolution ordering the Ten Commandments to be "posted in 'a very high traffic area' of [state] courthouse[s]." McCreary County complied, displaying a "large, gold-framed cop[y] of an abridged text of the King James version of the Ten Commandments, including a citation to the Book of Exodus." The American Civil Liberties Union of Kentucky almost immediately filed a lawsuit against the display, protesting that it unconstitutionally promoted religion. But before a federal district court could entertain that question, the Kentucky legislature passed another resolution directing counties to expand their displays with smaller copies of religious and historical documents. McCreary's expanded display included a statement "in remembrance and honor of Jesus Christ, the Prince of Ethics," the Mayflower Compact, the Declaration of Independence's "All men are endowed by their Creator" passage, and President Ronald Reagan's proclamation marking 1983 the "Year of the Bible." Curiously, it did *not* include the U.S. or Kentucky state constitutions.

The ACLU challenged the second display and a federal district court ordered in May 2000 that it be disassembled "IMMEDIATELY" and no government official was to "erect or cause to be erected similar displays." The County again changed the display by adding "framed copies of the Magna Carta, the [entire] Declaration of Independence, the Bill of Rights, the lyrics of the Star Spangled Banner . . . the National Motto, the Preamble to the Kentucky Constitution, and a picture of Lady Justice." It slapped a label on the display, "The Foundations of American Law and Government Display," and explained the alleged legal and historical significance of each document; the ACLU returned to court for a third time.

The case made its way to the U.S. Supreme Court, where the state ACLU affiliate argued that the display (in both its previous and current forms) failed *Lemon*'s "secular purpose" test. A five-justice majority agreed in June 2005. Opinion author Justice David Souter affirmed the importance of government neutrality in all religious matters, citing the rancor of contemporary debates over the role of religion in American politics. "[T]he divisiveness of religion in current public life is inescapable," he wrote. "This is no time to deny the prudence of the [First Amendment] to require the Government to stay neutral on religious belief, which is reserved for the conscience of the individual."

The decisions in *Van Orden* and *McCreary* were fractured and caustic. Individual justices wrote separately in both cases, often using his or her dissenting opinion as a soapbox to lament the majority's holding. True to form, Justice Antonin Scalia was the most acerbic. His dissenting opinion in *McCreary,* which he took the rare step of reading from the bench when the decisions came down on June 27, 2005, evoked the terrorist attacks of September 11, 2001, and retorted that the majority's decision "ratchets up this Court's hostility to religion." He further suggested that maybe religious liberty *should* be submitted to a majority vote. Responding to Justice John Paul Stevens's assertion in *Van Orden* that erecting state-sponsored Ten Commandments displays "'marginaliz[es] the belief systems of more than 7 million Americans' who adhere to religions that are not monotheistic," Scalia said they were not in the majority, and were therefore largely irrelevant to the "interest of the overwhelming majority of religious believers in being able to give God thanks and supplication *as a people*" (i.e., government actions on behalf of the people).

Van Orden and *McCreary* were significant in the their own right, but drew increased attention from Court watchers because they followed closely on the heels of a major Ten Commandments decision, played out in an epic saga involving the chief justice of Alabama, a 2.6-ton granite monument, the Religious Right, and the U.S. Supreme Court.

Alabama judge Roy Moore is a sort of celebrity spokesman for the Decalogue's public display. He achieved legendary status in 1995 when he refused to remove a plaque of the Ten Commandments from his Etowah County courtroom. Two lawsuits were filed challenging the plaque's prominent position in the courtroom, but both were dismissed on technical grounds.

Moore was then elected chief justice of the Alabama Supreme Court in 2001. In fact, he rode the controversy's coattails into office, promising to pay homage to the Ten Commandments in the building that housed the state's highest court. True to his word, he installed a 2.6-ton granite statue of the Ten Commandments in the state judicial building's rotunda late on the night of July 31, 2001. Americans United for Separation of Church and State, the ACLU of Alabama, and the Southern Poverty Law Center sued, and by November 2002 a federal court had ordered the monument's immediate removal. As was his right, Moore appealed but had no better luck in any higher court.

The U.S. Supreme Court finally refused to hear Moore's case, letting stand the lower court's ruling against the state-sponsored monument. In a striking display of contempt for the Constitution he had repeatedly sworn to uphold, Moore refused to remove the monolith, forcing his colleagues on the state Supreme Court to order the building manager to remove the monument immediately. The legal drama came to an end in late 2003 when the Alabama Court of the Judiciary removed him from office for violating the Alabama Canons of Judicial Ethics. Today, Moore and his monument are on tour around the United States. He is hailed as a hero by the Religious Right and has been a driving force behind keeping religious (i.e., Christian) displays on public property. In fact, he should be properly viewed as the worst kind of judge, one who puts his personal religious zeal ahead of the rule of law and the clear commands of the U.S. Constitution.

There is a test I have not yet discussed which is often used to evaluate the constitutionality of religious displays on public property. It is called the "endorsement test," and it is used to determine whether a government-sponsored action sanctions, or "endorses," religion. The test was developed by Justice Sandra Day O'Connor in *Lynch v. Donnelly,* a 1984 case considering a holiday display comprising a Christmas tree, a nativity scene, and a "Season's Greetings" banner in Pawtucket, Rhode Island. In her concurring opinion, which ultimately upheld the display as constitutional, Justice O'Connor stressed the importance of examining a government action's intended purpose and its actual effect. It was clear, in her view, that Pawtucket did not intend to endorse Christianity by including a crèche in the annual holiday display and that the "overall holiday setting" sent a message of seasonal celebration to viewers. Justice O'Connor made it clear that a purely religious holiday, which sent the message that some in the community were "insiders" and others were "outsiders," whether intentional or not, would violate her endorsement test and the Establishment Clause.

The endorsement test was applied in a similar case only five years after *Lynch.* In *Allegheny v. ACLU of Pennsylvania,* the Court used the test to consider the constitutionality of two holiday displays in Allegheny County, Pennsylvania. The first, displayed prominently in the county courthouse, featured an elaborate nativity scene adorned with a banner reading "Gloria in Excelsis Deo," that is, "Glory to God in the Highest." The second, an eighteen-foot menorah and forty-five-foot Christmas tree, was set up next to the City and County Building. The Court struck down the former and upheld the latter. While *Allegheny's* dual-faith display and *Lynch's* mixed secular-religious display did not necessarily convey endorsement of a particular religion, the Court reasoned, *Allegheny's* stand-alone nativity scene and religious message did.

OF MONKEYS AND MEN

Many Americans' exposure to the battles over the teaching of evolution in public schools has been through the popular portrayal of the 1925 Scopes "monkey trial." The proceeding, made famous by the play and movie *Inherit the Wind*, determined if public school teacher John Scopes had violated Tennessee's Butler Act, which banned "teach[ing] any theory that denies the story of the Divine Creation of man as taught in the Bible, and to teach instead that man has descended from a lower order of animals." The trial pitted Clarence Darrow and William Jennings Bryan, two of the twentieth century's most talented advocates, against each other. *Inherit the Wind* depicts a battle of the titans, with Darrow emerging as the clear winner in the popular mind, even though Scopes was ultimately convicted of violating the Butler Act. Contrary to popular belief, *Tennessee v. Scopes* never made it to the U.S. Supreme Court; the Tennessee Supreme Court vacated Scopes's conviction on procedural grounds in 1926.

Over forty years would pass before the U.S. Supreme Court heard the first case on teaching evolution in public schools. In *Epperson v. Arkansas,* the Court ruled that a state law prohibiting instruction that "mankind ascended or descended from a lower order of animals" was unconstitutional because it violated the Establishment Clause. The Clause, as the Court had previously ruled, calls not only for government neutrality between religions, but also neutrality between religion and nonreligion. Justice Abe Fortas wrote for a unanimous Court that Arkansas' "anti-evolution" act violated the *Lemon* test because it lacked a clear secular purpose. Fortas noted that Arkansas lawmakers had cleverly omitted Tennessee's reference to "the story of the Divine Creation of man as taught in the Bible." "[B]ut," he concluded, "there is no doubt that the motivation for the law was the same: to suppress the teaching of a theory which, it was thought, 'denied' the divine creation of man."

Of course, battles over creationism and evolution in public schools didn't end there; the Court heard a similar case in 1987. Recognizing that it could not ban outright the teaching of evolution, the Louisiana state legislature in 1981 passed a "Balanced Treatment Act." The act stated that while no public school teacher was required to present material on the origins of humanity, "creation science" and evolution must be given equal treatment if the topic was tackled. High school biology teacher Dan Aguillard challenged the law on behalf of himself and a group of parents and religious leaders. The U.S. Supreme Court invalidated the act in *Edwards v. Aguillard,* again noting that it had no secular purpose.

Justice William Brennan wrote for the majority that, similar to Arkansas' "anti-evolution" act, Louisiana's Balanced Treatment Act "is designed either to promote the theory of creation science which embodies a particular religious tenet by requiring that creation science be taught whenever evolution is taught or to prohibit the teaching of a scientific theory disfavored by certain religious sects by forbidding the teaching of evolution when creation science is not also taught. The Establishment Clause, however, 'forbids alike the preference of a religious doctrine or the prohibition of theory which is deemed antagonistic to a particular religious dogma.' Because the primary purpose of the [Act] is to advance a particular religious belief, the Act advances religion in violation of the Establishment Clause."

After suffering a series of losses over the teaching of evolution in public schools, some leaders in the Religious Right's creationism movement regrouped, and began advancing a theory they called "intelligent design," or ID. The theory states that living organisms, especially human beings, are so complex that they could not have possibly evolved by "natural selection," the mechanism explained nearly 150 years ago in Charles Darwin's *Origin of Species.* Life, they say, must be a creation of an "intelligent designer." Speaking before general audiences, ID proponents claim the "designer" could be anything from God to a space alien, but speaking behind closed doors, they readily admit that the designer is the God described in the Book of Genesis.

In 2004, the Dover, Pennsylvania, School Board became the first in the nation to adopt a science curriculum indirectly promoting intelligent design. A group of parents represented by Americans United for Separation of Church and State, the ACLU of Pennsylvania, and the law firm of Pepper Hamilton challenged the plan to tell ninth grade students that copies of a book about ID, described as a "scientific alternative" to the theory of evolution they were about to study, were available in the school's library. The textbooks, entitled

Of Pandas and People, they failed to mention, were donated by a local fundamentalist Christian church in an attempt to get religiously based creationism back into public school science classrooms.

The case went to trial on September 26, 2005, and concluded on November 4 of the same year. American United's intent was to show that the ID statement violated the Establishment Clause because the board lacked a secular purpose in adopting it. Our lawyers walked the court through three years of the school board's history, demonstrating how board members who were bent on getting creationism and school prayer back into the classroom accomplished part of their goal with the ID statement. They cited at length the Wedge Document, which is the Discovery Institute's (a leading ID think tank in Seattle, Washington) strategy for reintroducing religiously based creationism into public schools. The document states that the movement's goal is to "defeat scientific materialism and its destructive moral, cultural, and political legacies" and "to replace materialistic explanations with the theistic understanding that nature and human beings are created by God." Law professor Phillip Johnson, largely considered the father of the intelligent design movement, said of ID in 1996, "This isn't really, and never has been a debate about science. It's about religion and philosophy."

The joint legal team had a slam-dunk case in proving that the statement lacked a secular purpose, but they also felt it necessary to show how the statement, in the students' eyes at least, endorsed religion. (It should be noted that the school district objected to the court using the endorsement test because it felt it only applied to religious display cases. The court's opinion correctly pointed out that both the *Lemon* and the endorsement tests were appropriate standards for this case.) The simple fact that the statement flowed from school officials was enough to convince any reasonable student that the school endorsed its content.

The decision from U.S. District Court judge John E. Jones III came on December 20, 2005. It was remarkable. Every detail, every excuse, every piece of evidence that was exposed during the forty-day trial was painstakingly analyzed in Jones's 139-page opinion. The court concluded that the ID policy did indeed fail *Lemon*'s secular purpose test, and chided the board for misleading it and the Dover community. The school board's "flagrant and insulting falsehoods to the Court," Judge Jones wrote, "provide sufficient and compelling evidence for us that any allegedly secular purposes that have been offered in support of the ID Policy are equally insincere." Jones also noted that the statement failed the endorsement test by sending a message to students that the district doubted the validity of a scientifically sound theory, and by "present[ing] students with a religious alternative masquerading as a scientific theory, direct[ing] them to consult a creationist text as though it were a science resource, and instruct[ing] students to forego scientific inquiry in the public school classroom and instead to seek out religious instruction elsewhere."

Each school board member who approved the unconstitutional statement, all but one of whom was up for reelection in 2005, had been voted out of office just one month before the decision came down. They were replaced by a slate of residents who campaigned on returning scientific integrity to the area's public schools by repealing the ID statement. *Kitzmiller v. Dover Area School District* was not appealed to a higher court. The path-breaking decision has served as a guide for courts and school districts considering ID curricula around the country. Indeed, in early 2006, it caused a school board in Lebec, California to drop an elective class in "The Philosophy of Design," which taught almost nothing but antievolution propaganda. In 2007, the decision influenced school boards in Kansas and Ohio to abandon plans to include "alternatives" to evolution in statewide high school biology curricula.

TAXES AND TUITION

Vouchers are state-subsidized private school tuition grants. Parents in states with voucher schemes are given a slip of paper they can "cash in" at the participating school of their choice. Voucher proponents hail the schemes as a way to get children (especially low-income and minority children) out of "failing" public schools. Improving our national public education system is a noble and necessary goal, but not every method of trying to do this is necessarily constitutional. Vouchers redeemed at religious schools raise serious concerns about the separation of church and state.

Religious schools are inherently religious. It sounds obvious, but it's worth remembering that religious belief, teaching, and practice permeate life at a religious school. Most private religious and parochial schools require students to attend worship, study the school's faith, and comply with its doctrinal teachings. Indeed, many of these schools exist precisely because parents want a religious alternative to secular public education. Our Constitution has protected parents' right to educate their children in private schools since the previously mentioned *Pierce* decision in 1925, but it has protected taxpayers' right not to fund religious education and institutions since 1791. I don't think we should forget that.

The Supreme Court took up the question of direct public aid to religious schools and parents of children in those schools long before the current voucher schemes were hatched. In *Committee for Public Education and Religious Liberty v. Nyquist*, a fractured majority ruled that New York could not pay for the upkeep of religious schools or reimburse parents for sending their children to parochial and other private religious schools. The Establishment Clause simply forbids laws advancing religion, regardless of whatever "social good" they might theoretically bring.

Nyquist was decided in 1973. The Court heard a number of cases dealing with direct and indirect public aid to private religious schools in the following thirty years, and the *Nyquist* principle banning all forms of such aid gradually deteriorated over that time. *Zelman v. Simmons-Harris* capped *Nyquist's* decline in 2001 by allowing parents in Cleveland, Ohio, to use vouchers to bankroll their children's education at parochial and other private schools.

Americans United and its allies challenged the voucher plan in Cleveland that resulted in 95 percent of participating children attending religious schools. The federal district court and court of appeals accepted the argument that the program unconstitutionally advanced religion, deciding that "the voucher program has the primary effect of advancing religion, and that it constitutes an endorsement of religion and sectarian education in violation of the Establishment Clause." Our luck changed when we reached the nation's highest court.

The Supreme Court upheld the program five votes to four. Although the justices in the minority believed that the flow of funds to religious educational institutions had the "principal or primary effect" of advancing religion, and that the law "foster[ed] an excessive government entanglement with religion," the Court was able to cobble together five votes for the opposing view. The majority disagreed with the lower court that the "program is designed in a manner calculated to attract religious institutions and chooses the beneficiaries of aid by non-neutral criteria." Rather, the Court concluded that the "program is one of true private choice," allowing parents to choose from equally acceptable secular and religious schools. It also noted, as it had before, that aid did not flow directly from the government to the religious institution, but from the government, to an independent actor, to the school of the actor's choice. The Court did stress, however, that constitutional voucher programs could not provide direct aid to religious schools, could not include schools that discriminated based on religion, race, or ethnicity, and must be "neutral in all respects toward religion."

Justice Sandra Day O'Connor wrote separately, taking pains to stress the importance of secular choices. She was "persuaded," she wrote in this case, that the "Cleveland voucher program affords parents of eligible children genuine nonreligious options and is consistent with the Establishment Clause." Unless "beneficiaries of indirect aid have a genuine choice among religious and nonreligious organizations when determining the organization to which they will direct that aid," she wrote, "the program should be struck down under the Establishment Clause." She concluded that available programs must be acceptable substitutes for one another. Justice O'Connor's concurrence will carry significant weight when future federal courts weigh the constitutionality of "faith-based initiatives."

Faith-based initiatives are similar to school vouchers in that they funnel government funds to religious organizations to provide social services. I will discuss them further in the section called No Religious Discrimination, but note here that many critics believe such grants are not distributed evenhandedly among religious groups or between religious and secular programs. Therefore, secular programs may not exist in some areas to serve as alternatives to religious programs receiving taxpayer money. It will be interesting to see if the former justice's concern for equality is borne in mind as the Supreme Court becomes increasingly divided along ideological lines.

Curiously, the *Zelman* decision did not lead to many new voucher initiatives. State supreme courts in Colorado and Florida declared voucher schemes unconstitutional under various provisions of those states' constitutions. Thirty-six state constitutions do appear to contain strict limitations on taxpayer funding for religiously affiliated institutions, and are likely to be the core of future battles.

USING PUBLIC SCHOOL BUILDINGS FOR RELIGIOUS EXTRACURRICULAR ACTIVITIES

Controversies over church-state separation proliferated during President Ronald Reagan's administration. The president himself unsuccessfully advocated for public subsidies for religious schools, and even tried to convince Congress to amend the Constitution to permit state-sponsored prayer once again. Those drastic moves failed, but the Religious Right was able to secure a "compromise" in the Equal Access Act of 1984. The act banned public schools from regulating students' extracurricular meetings on the basis of the participants' religious, political, or philosophical opinions or speech. The Supreme Court upheld the act eight votes to one in 1990.

Over time, the Equal Access Act has cut both ways for the Religious Right. In 1998, Michah White wanted to form an atheist club at his Grand Blanc, Michigan, public high school. School officials forbade it, saying instead he could form a club to study comparative religion. White found the "compromise" unacceptable and contacted Americans United for help. AU negotiated a solution that allowed White to form the club he wanted—which, given the ensuing controversy, generated much more interest than it would likely have drawn had he simply been given the go-ahead in the first place. Similarly, the "equal access" principle has been the basis for allowing Gay-Straight Student Alliances all over the country (although a federal district court in 2004 allowed a Lubbock, Texas, public high school to bar an alliance from meeting or advertising on campus).

The Supreme Court heard another equal access case three years later, this time dealing with the right of outside groups to use public school facilities. In *Lamb's Chapel v. Center Moriches Free Union School District,* the Court ruled that a New York school district's refusal to allow a church-based group to use school facilities to show a Christian film series violated the church's free speech rights because many other secular groups had been granted permission for similar events in the past. The discriminatory policy didn't violate the group's free exercise rights per se because it didn't prohibit the group from practicing its religion. However, the Court concluded that "viewpoint discrimination," where the government picks and chooses groups to interact with based on their viewpoints, can unconstitutionally impact religious groups.

"Viewpoint discrimination" surfaced again in the 1995 case *Rosenberger v. University of Virginia. Rosenberger* considered whether a public university, which had a vested interest in avoiding an Establishment Clause violation, could refuse to provide student activity funds to a Christian student newspaper. University policy denied any funding to a student organization that "primarily promotes or manifests a particular belief in or about a deity or an ultimate reality." The students sued, arguing that the university could not withhold student activity funds just because of the requesting organization's viewpoint and that the funds in question weren't really "taxpayer dollars" because students had willingly paid them. Five justices agreed with the students on both counts. If a public educational institution agreed to fund one student organization, it must agree to fund any law-abiding student organization. In weighing students' free speech rights against the university's obligation to the Establishment Clause, the Court concluded, "[t]he violation following from the University's denial of [financial] support...is not excused by the necessity of complying with the Establishment Clause." Four justices disagreed, concluding that "[t]he Court today, for the first time, approves direct funding of core religious activities by an arm of the State." In response to the majority's conclusion that the funds in question were not public funds because they had been acquired via student activity fees, the minority wrote "there is no warrant for distinguishing among public funding sources for purposes of applying the First Amendment's prohibition of religious establishment. [We] would hold that the University's refusal to support petitioners' religious activities is compelled by the Establishment Clause."

Another case dealing with outside groups in public schools came in 2001. An evangelical Christian group called the Good News Club wanted to conduct religious education classes in a New York public elementary school just minutes after the school day ended. A number of church-state separation advocacy groups supported parents who were concerned that their elementary-age children would not be able to differentiate between a private and school-sponsored meeting if the club met so soon after the students were dismissed for the day. The groups, including Americans United, filed friend-of-the-court briefs arguing this point in Good News Club v. Milford Central School District. The club, on the other hand, claimed that the school district's blanket ban on renting school facilities to religious groups violated its free speech rights. The Supreme Court agreed with the club.

The Court's shifting stance toward government interaction with religion is evident in its decision favoring the Good News Club's "viewpoint discrimination" claim. Tellingly, the majority opinion was authored by Justice Clarence Thomas, an outspoken proponent of states' (currently unconstitutional) power to establish an official religion. Justice David Souter's dissent took his colleagues to task for failing to recognize the Good News Club for what it really was. The majority characterized the club as one with a religious view on an otherwise secular subject (e.g., morality). In reality, Justice Souter concluded, Good News Club's purpose was to evangelize and convert; they told children that they would go to hell if they did not accept Christ and urged them to "correct" their parents, lest they be absent from heaven. He argued that the Milford School District could exclude the Club from using its space because its *behavior*, not its viewpoint, set it apart from other groups allowed to use the space.

Justice Souter warned the nation that "This case would stand for the remarkable proposition that any public school opened for civic meetings must be opened for use as a church, synagogue, or mosque." The justice's fear has not yet been tested at the nation's highest court.

"Viewpoint discrimination" isn't something only public school officials worry about; all government officials must confront the issue when regulating private speech and expression on public property. We Americans are very fortunate that we're allowed to celebrate our religious beliefs in public; our public squares are not naked (as some Religious Right leaders claim), but full of diverse religious symbols, festivals, and expression. I mentioned earlier that the place of religious symbols in the public square has long symbolized the underlying tension between the right to religious expression and the need for church-state separation. Contributing to this tension is a false assumption on which many Religious Right leaders based their arguments that they are "persecuted" for expressing their religious beliefs in public. Indeed, they falsely assume that our Constitution treats religion in precisely the same way it treats other ideas and activities. In fact, it does not. "Congress shall make no law respecting an establishment of religion..." has no counterpart elsewhere in the Constitution that prohibits established cultural, political, or economic ideas. Therefore, the government has an interest in disallowing government-sponsored religious expression or allowing activity that implies government endorsement or disapproval of religion. Here's an example of the state denying religious expression on public property because it was obligated to abide by the Establishment Clause. In November 1993, the Ku Klux Klan wanted to erect a giant wooden cross on the public plaza abutting the Ohio statehouse in Columbus. The Capitol Square Review Board, the committee responsible for the public space, denied the group's request on Establishment Clause grounds. The board argued that it was obligated to avoid actually or effectively endorsing religion. Naturally, the City of Columbus was concerned that people would think it had put up the giant cross, and therefore endorsed Christianity.

The KKK sued, alleging that the state had engaged in unconstitutional "viewpoint discrimination" by denying the display. The group won at every level, from the district court all the way up to the U.S. Supreme Court. Justice Antonin Scalia delivered the Court's split decision two years later in *Capitol Square Review Board v. Pinette*. The majority ruled that by opening up the public forum to private groups, the City of Columbus was opening it up to any private group. It could regulate private displays, but only if it served "a compelling state interest" (i.e., the state had a really, really good reason) and the regulation was as narrow as possible. A three-justice plurality led by Justice Scalia determined that the state was not at risk of violating the so-called endorsement test by allowing the KKK to erect its freestanding cross near the statehouse. Justice Scalia is no fan of the endorsement test, so it's not surprising he concluded the state didn't show a good enough reason to deny the KKK's display. Justices David Souter, Sandra Day O'Connor, and Stephen Breyer concluded that the city shouldn't have banned the display outright. For them, a sign on the display simply noting that it was privately sponsored would have done the trick.

Justices John Paul Stevens and Ruth Bader Ginsberg protested that the state had shown a "compelling" reason to reject the freestanding cross. "The Establishment Clause," Justice Stevens wrote, "should be construed to create a strong presumption against the installation of unattended religious symbols on public property." He concluded that the cross violated the endorsement test because the "unquestionably religious symbol" may have sent conflicting messages to passersby. "Some might have perceived it as a message of love, others as a message of hate, still others as a message of exclusion—a statehouse sign calling powerfully to mind their outsider status. In any event, it was a message that the state of Ohio may not communicate to its citizens without violating the Establishment Clause." Justice Ginsberg continued in her own dissent, "If the aim of the Establishment Clause is genuinely to uncouple government from church ... [then] a State may not permit, and a court may not order, a display of this character."

STANDING TO SUE

Many people believe that a lawsuit can solve any legal problem. Litigation is the customary way of resolving disputes in this country, but there are certain limits on who can file a lawsuit. Four basic rules must be met before a case can go forward:

First, a plaintiff must reasonably demonstrate actual or imminent injury. That is, he has to show that the contested action or program has harmed or will imminently harm himself or his interests. Thinking that a program *might* cause harm or just disliking the program does not give someone the right to contest it in court. Also, being a taxpayer is typically not reason enough to challenge funding of a contested action or program.

Second, a plaintiff must show "causation." He must give the court reason to believe that his actual or imminent injury is causally connected to the contested action or program. Third, a plaintiff must show that there is some reasonable chance of undoing the harm caused by the contested action or program if the case goes to trial. Finally, a plaintiff must show that his complaint addresses a current action or program. A case that cannot be tried because it targets an expired action or program is usually declared "moot."

The one exception to the injury and causation requirements involves government funding of religion. In a 1968 case called *Flast v. Cohen,* the Supreme Court decided that being a taxpayer was enough to pursue legal action against Establishment Clause violations. At issue in this landmark case was a provision in the Elementary and Secondary Education Act of 1965 allowing Congress to "finance instruction and the purchase of educational materials for use in religious and sectarian schools." A group of taxpayers, having no connection to the act other than that their dollars would fund its implementation, challenged the provision as unconstitutional. The Court did not rule on the question's merits, but the taxpayers walked away with a victory nonetheless. In *Flast*, the Court carved out this special "taxpayer standing" exception because the Establishment Clause's primary purpose is to bar government-funded religious institutions, education, and practice. The Court allowed taxpayer standing in cases involving congressionally appropriated direct aid to religious institutions, but it has not extended the exception to cases involving indirect aid such as government land grants.

In 1988, the Court also acknowledged "standing" for a group of federal taxpayers, clergy, and the American Jewish Congress, who challenged the constitutionality of the Adolescent Family Life Act. The act authorized the Department of Health and Human Services to distribute grants for sex education and research to public or nonprofit private organizations or agencies in the area of premarital adolescent sexual relations and pregnancy. The act forbade grantees from talking about birth control or abortion, a condition on federal grants that is common in conservative administrations. The Court in *Bowen v. Kendrick* recognized that the taxpayers had standing to challenge the apportionment, since the aid flowed directly from Congress to the executive agency to the grantee. It did not, however, decide that the act was unconstitutional on its face, as the petitioners had hoped. The act, the Court found, satisfied all three of *Lemon*'s requirements; it neither lacked a secular purpose, advanced religion, nor fostered excessive entanglement between government and religion.

Nearly two decades later, the Court considered a case not unlike *Bowen v. Kendrick*. The case was *Hein v. Freedom from Religion Foundation*, a case in which Americans United participated as a friend of the court. As it was in *Bowen*, the *Hein* Court was tasked with determining whether a group of taxpayers had standing to challenge a program created and implemented by the executive branch. The programs at issue in *Hein* were President George W. Bush's White House Office of Faith-Based and Community Initiatives and several related programs promoting its objective. President Bush created the office through an executive order in 2001, so it has never received direct funding by Congress; it's paid for out of the executive branch's annual budget. Congress may not have directly appropriated the money, but our tax dollars were used to fund it nonetheless, the taxpayers argued. The case did not challenge the office or its programs on their face; we just wanted to know if taxpayers would be allowed to get their feet in the courthouse door. Five members of the Court said they did not have a right to sue in this case.

CONCLUSION

Of all the cases I've discussed, I want to bring us back to the two that are the bedrock of constitutional law on religion. *Everson v. Board of Education* extended the Federal Constitution's ban on laws or actions "respecting an establishment of religion" to the states. *Everson* is the single most important case in this area of law because it forbids all levels of government from imposing or restricting religion. The second, *Lemon v. Kurtzman,* is important because it was the first case to provide a standard method for determining if a law or government action "established" religion. Almost every church-state separation case since 1971 has relied on *Lemon.* It has never been overturned, but there has been a shift away from *Lemon*'s three-prong test in recent years. As we saw in the government-sponsored religious display cases, the Supreme Court's tendency is to ask if government-sponsored religious expression "endorses" rather than "promotes" or "advances" religion. For all practical purposes, though, there may not be a real difference between the three labels. *Lemon* and its progeny remain useful in evaluating church-state violations today. However, a few sitting Supreme Court justices have advocated scrapping *Lemon.* These extremely conservative jurists prefer the "coercion test," which I discussed in the school prayer cases, over *Lemon*'s "secular purpose," "primary or principal effect," and "excessive entanglement" and *Lynch v. Donnelly's* "endorsement" tests. The Establishment Clause, they say, only bars compelled religious practice, belief, and financial support.

So, that's how we got to where we are today on what most Americans consider church-state separation's "core" issues. In fact, Americans have more religious freedom than any people in world history. The ability to choose what to believe, whether and how to worship, and what to teach our children are not privileges, but inalienable rights guaranteed by the First Amendment to the U.S. Constitution.

Those so-called black-robed, unelected federal judges and the courts on which they sit are charged with protecting these most sacred rights. They have not "kicked God out of public life," as the Religious Right claims. Quite the contrary, they have preserved Christians', and indeed all Americans', right to express their beliefs in public. As should be obvious by now, I think the Court has sometimes gone too far in protecting Christians' rights at the expense of religious minorities. It baffles me how the Religious Right can look at cases like *Cantwell, Van Orden, Lynch, Zelman, Lamb's Chapel, Rosenberger, Good News Club,* and *Pinette* and still say that their followers are "persecuted."

As we'll discover in the pages that follow, there is a wealthy and well-organized movement afoot to completely dismantle the wall between church and state. I would ask each of its members, and you, too, as you read this book, to answer a question Justice Sandra Day O'Connor posed in *McCreary County v. ACLU:* "Why would we trade a system that has served us so well for one that has served others so poorly?"

In the forthcoming pages, I will discuss developments in the "core" issues I just mentioned. In addition, though, I'll explore how the Religious Right has an even broader agenda. As I said in my last book, *Piety & Politics,* "It seems the Religious Right wants to run your life from the moment of conception until the moment of death (which they will define), as well as virtually every minute in between."

Current Religious Freedom Issues

END-OF-LIFE CARE

> *"As obvious as it may seem, one needs to look no further than the Ten Commandments for the timeless and controlling moral Principle to guide the outcome of [Terri Schiavo's] case: 'Thou shall not kill.'"*
>
> THE FAMILY RESEARCH COUNCIL
> POLICY STATEMENT, March 22, 2005

America treats death a lot like sex. Images of death often dominate our films and television screens, but we caricature the experience and we certainly don't like to discuss it in any serious fashion. Moreover, we don't want to consider it in advance of absolute necessity. We are uncomfortable filling out "living wills" and "durable powers of attorney" that give instructions, general or specific, about how our loved ones should make decisions in the event that we become incapable of making our own. Questions about life support, extraordinary medical care, and managing terminal illnesses are ethically complex and require a great deal of soul-searching and specific, often difficult, instructions to make sure our last wishes are honored.

Unfortunately, the Religious Right does not want us and our families to make these personal choices. Its leaders believe they have the only moral compass capable of dealing with these questions and, as we will see in this chapter, are willing and able to impose their wishes on us. Our discomfort leaves us vulnerable to their manipulation.

A particularly egregious example of this propensity arose in the case of Ms. Terri Schiavo. Following an eight-year effort to revive his wife from a persistent vegetative state, Michael Schiavo petitioned a Florida court to remove the feeding tube sustaining Terri. Because Ms. Shiavo lacked a living will or directions for extraordinary medical intervention, she was assigned a *guardian ad litem* to act on her behalf in court. Questions over Ms. Schiavo's presumed wishes, Mr. Schiavo's right to make decisions, and her family's religious teachings were hashed out over five years and four separate cases in Florida courts.

What Ms. Schiavo, her husband, and her family endured during her fifteen-year ordeal was deeply personal but not uncommon. Families of people with critical medical conditions often disagree over the best treatment for their loved one, and they may turn to the courts to help them resolve legal matters concerning the person's care. Ms. Schiavo's case was unique, however, because the Religious Right, the United States Congress, and President George W. Bush rushed into the fray on her parents' behalf.

The Religious Right held Ms. Schiavo up as a poster child in their crusade to end the "culture of death." At a closed-door meeting with the Family Research Council in 2005, then House majority leader Tom DeLay (R-TX) said one thing "God has brought to us is Terri Schiavo, to elevate the visibility of what's going on in America..." DeLay said America's "culture of death" was "bigger than any one of us," but supporters had to do "everything that is in our power to save Terri Schiavo and anybody else that may be in this kind of position."

And act they did. DeLay convened Congress in an emergency weekend session to pass legislation to reopen the exhausted state court proceedings in federal courts, beginning with a brand new trial in federal district court. The legislation passed with much help from the Religious Right, and President Bush interrupted his summer vacation to sign the bill into law. Fortunately, federal courts blocked the congressional interference.

The Florida state courts consistently ruled in favor of Michael Schiavo's effort to discontinue artificial life support. Ms. Schiavo's feeding tube was removed for the third and final time on March 18, 2005; she died two weeks later, on March 31.

Terri Schiavo's tragic demise received unprecedented media attention and government involvement, but it did not establish a "right to die." It did illustrate, however, how important it is for each of us to discuss end-of-life care with our loved ones before it's too late. A medical decision made by a legally competent patient will always stand. When a patient is unable to think or speak for him- or herself, however, someone else has to be authorized to judge the merits of possible plans and make a decision. Under most state laws, including Florida's, the patient's spouse can make decisions to use or forgo any life-sustaining treatment unless there is evidence of malicious intent or disregard of the patient's well-being. Withholding food and water are universally considered in our legal system to be in the same category as taking a person off a respirator or other similar medical devices. Usually, such a case does not even go to court, though the courts are always available to adjudicate allegations of mistakes—as they were called upon to do, over and over, in the Schiavo case.

Ironically, the same cabal of right-wing groups that generally despise the federal judiciary sought to have the issue of medical decision making, traditionally a matter for the state courts, elevated to the federal judiciary. The federal courts, they thought, would be more sympathetic to their view that the individual does not have a right to determine his or her own medical destiny. This thinly veiled attempt to litigate the "culture of death" shows how hypocritical the Religious Right really is. They are not, as they profess, interested in legal philosophy and procedure, but in legal results.

Federal and state courts have rarely been involved in so-called right-to-die cases. The New Jersey Supreme Court in 1976 examined the case of twenty-two-year-old Karen Quinlan, who spent more than a year in a persistent vegetative state after she inexplicably lapsed into a coma. Her father sought to remove her from a respirator and faced opposition from some physicians and local right-to-life groups. The New Jersey Supreme Court eventually granted "guardianship" to Mr. Quinlan and ruled that he could act on her behalf to remove the artificial breathing apparatus under an extension of the "right to privacy" found by the Supreme Court in other cases involving intimate moral decisions. This right overrode any considerations used by lower courts to justify forced use of the respirator.

The U.S. Supreme Court heard its first right-to-die case in 1989. It reviewed the Missouri Supreme Court's decision to overturn a lower court ruling allowing Nancy Cruzan's family to remove the feeding tube keeping her alive. Cruzan had been in a "persistent vegetative state" since a devastating car accident seven years earlier, and the state Supreme Court determined that the lower court had not required "clear and convincing evidence" for discontinuing life support. Five justices agreed with that assessment in *Cruzan v. Director, Missouri Department of Health,* holding that a person has a constitutional right to refuse medical care, but the state can require people acting on a legally incompetent person's behalf to show "clear and convincing evidence" that he or she is acting on the patient's wishes. Otherwise, the Court reasoned, there are no safeguards against the patient's professed advocate from acting in his or her own self-interest.

The case was sent back to a Missouri court to be considered under the U.S. Supreme Court–approved standard of evidence in 1990. A judge again allowed Cruzan's family to disconnect her feeding tube and they did so on December 14; she passed away eleven days later, on December 26, 1990. Nancy Cruzan's gravestone today reads, "Born July 20, 1957, Departed Jan. 11, 1983, At Peace Dec. 26, 1990." In an especially sad ending to this story, her father bore a heavy burden of feeling that he had let his daughter down by dragging her case through the courts for so many years; he ended his own life a few years later, in 1996. It is not just the patient who suffers when these important decisions are delayed.

In 1997, the state of Oregon passed an initiative allowing competent, terminally ill persons to obtain drugs from doctors in order to end their lives. Its proponents call this "physician assistance in dying" because the doctor writes a prescription for a fatal dose of drugs and the patient then must fill the prescription and administer the dose to him- or herself. The patient must have a prognosis of likely death within six months and there are various safeguards such as a second physician opinion, a specific requirement to evaluate for psychological problems or coercion, and a two-week waiting period. The patient must be an adult who is competent and capable of taking the medications on his or her own. However, the patient does not have to have severe symptoms.

Critics of legal "physician assistance in dying" sometimes fear that if society makes it too simple or too commonplace for very sick, old, or dependent persons to end their lives, it will become socially accepted, and indeed, expected. That argument is frequently matched with the concern that such laws could curtail pressure to make changes in the overall health care system which would make pain relief and other symptom management reliably available to all citizens.

The choice to escape suffering near death by being continuously sedated is already legal, though many physicians are not skilled at managing deep sedation and many hospitals and nursing homes are uncomfortable allowing the procedure. Some disability rights groups insist that legalizing "physician assistance in dying" will eventually co-opt legally incompetent patients, and society's least-valued members will have little claim to the kind of support that would make life worth living.

The U.S. Supreme Court took up the issue of "physician assistance in dying" in *Vacco v. Quill* and *Washington v. Glucksberg,* decided together in 1997. The Court unanimously found no federal constitutional right to have physician assistance in suicide, but endorsed states' authority to legislate the issue. This democratic discretion was challenged a few years later when U.S. Attorney General John Ashcroft tried to stop Oregon doctors from writing otherwise legal prescriptions for fatal doses of drugs to end a terminally ill patient's life. The Justice Department argued that the drugs were controlled substances regulated by the federal Controlled Substances Act. The Supreme Court ruled 6–3 in early 2006 that the federal law did not give the Justice Department authority to punish physicians who legally prescribed lethal medications in accordance with Oregon's law.

Whether states should legalize "physician assistance in dying" and what protections and safeguards should be in place are complicated public policy issues because they require balancing free will with disadvantaged populations' vulnerability. However, it is quite clear that the issue should not be one more opportunity to enforce a particular religious view. People who find value in enduring pain, or spending every effort possible to live a little longer, should be able to do that. But people who have made peace with dying and mainly want to avoid suffering or overwhelming burdens on their family members should be able to forgo treatments and have reliable prevention and relief of pain, even if that means a shorter life.

The argument about how to provide services to those sick enough to die is important to have, and it is important to have it without claiming that the political process should adopt religiously based views that assume that women should be willing to give up their own life plans in order to provide care, or that people should find transcendent meaning in suffering.

REPRODUCTIVE HEALTH

> "Feminism discounts every bit of value the Lord has placed on living in relation to him. It's a movement that negates the pattern of marriage and the importance of children and men. It says that women can determine their own futures; they're stronger, they're smarter, they're better than men. They should be able to kill their children.... Everything that is ignoble is sanctioned."
> DIANE PASSNO, Executive Vice President,
> Focus on the Family, September 2000

> "I'm pro-choice. I think that women should have a choice over their bodies. I think it's very unfortunate that in this country especially

that we don't make it easier for those women who make the choice for life. But I don't agree at all with making abortions illegal just because a religion said so."

FIRST FREEDOM FIRST Focus Group Member, Albuquerque

"I say that we are all sovereign citizens cooperating together in a country. My husband doesn't get to tell me what to do. My government certainly doesn't."

FIRST FREEDOM FIRST Focus Group Member, Albuquerque

Some of the Religious Right's most familiar efforts are in the area of reproductive health. Its leaders label themselves as "pro-life" and are intent on passing laws that reflect that ideology. People as diverse as Democratic congressman Barney Frank and former Republican governor of Arkansas Mike Huckabee have opined that it seems the "pro-life" movement is only interested in life from the moment of conception to the moment of birth. Actually, it is now interested in the moment of death, too.

Surprisingly, the Religious Right's concern over reproductive health stretches beyond the U.S. Supreme Court's decision to legalize most abortions in 1973. Indeed, many abhor the Court's decision to legalize birth control for married couples in 1965.

In 1930, the state of Connecticut made it illegal for anyone to prescribe or use "drug[s], medicinal article[s] or instrument[s] for the purpose of preventing conception." Offenders were subject to a fine of at least $50, up to one year in jail, or both. The statute was challenged on its face in 1943 and 1961, but the Supreme Court ruled that plaintiffs lacked standing in both cases.

That changed when two of the plaintiffs, Estelle Griswold and Dr. C. Lee Buxton, opened a birth control clinic in New Haven, Connecticut. They wanted to challenge the law. Their intent was to be arrested and convicted for violating the statute, and then to challenge its constitutionality all the way to the nation's highest court. They succeeded four years later in *Griswold v. Connecticut*.

The seven-justice majority concluded that the right to marital privacy was protected by the Fourteenth Amendment to the Constitution. The high court's explanation leaned heavily on Justice John Marshall Harlan's dissent contesting the court's dismissal of the 1961 case, *Poe v. Ullman.* "[T]he full scope of the liberty guaranteed by the [Fourteenth Amendment] cannot be found in or limited by the precise terms of the specific guarantees elsewhere provided in the Constitution," he wrote. "This 'liberty' is not a series of isolated points pricked out in terms of the taking of property; the freedom of speech, press, and religion; the right to keep and bear arms; the freedom from unreasonable searches and seizures; and so on. It is a rational continuum which, broadly speaking, includes a freedom from all substantial arbitrary impositions and purposeless restraints."

The Constitution's silence on personal relationships does not exclude their protection from the document's purview. Writing for the majority, Justice William O. Douglas cited several First and Fourteenth Amendment cases dealing with inherent constitutional rights. The Court had previously determined that the right to educate one's child (*Pierce v. Society of Sisters,* 1925), to learn a foreign language (*Meyer v. Nebraska,* 1923), and to choose one's own associates (*NAACP v. Alabama,* 1958) were all absent from, but implicitly protected by, the First and Fourteenth Amendments.

Privacy rights also arise elsewhere in the Bill of Rights. The Third, Fourth, and Fifth Amendments had been used before 1965 to protect privacy in the home and in public life. *Boyd v. United States,* for example, recognized in 1886 that the Fourth and Fifth Amendments protected against governmental invasions "of the sanctity of a man's home and the privacies of life." Government actions violating the Third Amendment (no forcibly quartering soldiers in private homes during peacetime) have never been considered by the U.S. Supreme Court, but the U.S. Second Court of Appeals in 1982 concluded that "[t]he Third Amendment was designed to assure a fundamental right to privacy." The Ninth Amendment also supports this argument by barring the government from trampling rights and liberties just because they're not explicitly mentioned in the Constitution.

So why does all this legalistic talk matter? Because privacy is at the heart of reproductive freedom. What rights do you have if you don't have the right to direct your most personal and intimate family decisions? Most people resolve these matters by discussing them with their spouse or significant other and then turn to others for support, often members of the clergy. Since there isn't one "religious" opinion on matters of reproductive health, why shouldn't these decision-making processes be left completely to the individual and her chosen advisors? Variations of those questions appear repeatedly in Supreme Court cases dealing with reproductive health, and the Religious Right fights personal autonomy, opting instead to impose its religious views on the sensitive subject every time.

The Supreme Court next considered reproductive health and privacy rights in 1972. The Court concluded in *Eisenstadt v. Baird* that laws regulating reproductive health could not treat married and unmarried people differently, thereby invalidating a Massachusetts law barring doctors from dispensing and unmarried people from using birth control. Justice William Brennan wrote for the six-justice majority, "If the right of privacy means anything, it is the right of the individual, married or single, to be free from unwarranted governmental intrusion into matters so fundamentally affecting a person as the decision whether to bear or beget a child."

The Religious Right as we know it today was hardly a twinkle in its founders' eyes when *Griswold* and *Eisenstadt* were decided. Therefore, power players active in today's "pro-life" debate said little, if anything, of the two cases overturning anticontraception laws. They have, however, picked up *Griswold* and *Eisenstadt* as tools in their quest to overturn their most famous progeny, *Roe v. Wade*. Christian Coalition founder and TV preacher Pat Robertson said to a 1997 Coalition gathering, *Griswold* "was made up out of whole cloth" and "I want to see it abolished." So basically, the good reverend has no problem with the government cozying up between you and your mate in your marriage bed. I would characterize that thought as, to use a nonlegal term, "extremely creepy."

Most people have heard of *Roe v. Wade*, the case that legalized most abortions in 1973. It's still a hot topic in political debates and it's practically the only case some people want judicial nominees to discuss. Indeed, abortion is the single issue that has both galvanized support from conservative religious voters and propelled the Religious Right to power within the Republican Party.

Roe is indeed an important case, but there are two other abortion cases I'd like to discuss because they shed a bright light on the Religious Right's agenda. The first is *Webster v. Reproductive Health Services*. In 1989, a fractured Supreme Court majority upheld a Missouri statute restricting abortions performed by public employees or paid for by public funds. Interestingly, the Court overlooked the statute's religious flair in the preamble's assertion that "[t]he life of each human being begins at conception."

Only Justice John Paul Stevens objected that the definition violated the First Amendment Establishment Clause. In an eloquent dissent, citing Americans United's friend-of-the-court brief, Justice Stevens concluded that the definition lacked any secular (e.g., scientific) support. "There is unquestionably a theological basis for such a [definition], just as there was unquestionably a theological basis for the Connecticut statute that the Court invalidated in *Griswold*. Our jurisprudence, however, has consistently required a secular basis for valid legislation." He continued, explaining why the statute endorsed, not merely coincided with, a religious belief. "This conclusion does not, and could not, rest on the fact that the [definition of life] happens to coincide with the tenets of certain religions.... Rather, it rests on the fact that the [definition], an unequivocal endorsement of a religious tenet by some but by no means all Christian faiths, serves no identifiable secular purpose. That fact alone compels a conclusion that the statute violates the Establishment Clause."

Justice Stevens also recognized a very familiar phenomenon rarely cited in Supreme Court decisions. "Bolstering my conclusion" he wrote, "is the fact that the intensely divisive character of much of the national debate over the abortion issue reflects the deeply held religious convictions of many of the participants of the debate. The Missouri Legislature may not inject its endorsement of a particular religious tradition into this debate...." Justice Stevens hit the nail on the head! Religious belief is central to the debate over reproductive health. Reproductive choice proponents need to make this connection clear. Justice Stevens may have dissented from *Webster,* but one case's dissent can easily become another's majority opinion on more enlightened courts.

The second case is *Planned Parenthood of Pennsylvania v. Casey.* In 1992, a deeply split Supreme Court upheld *Roe*'s basic holding that a woman has a limited right to terminate a pregnancy but also upheld several restrictions on the procedure. For the first time the Court devised a standard for determining if a restriction was unconstitutional under *Roe:* restrictions cannot purposely or effectively impose an "undue burden" on a woman seeking the otherwise legal procedure. An "undue burden," the three-justice plurality concluded, is a "substantial obstacle in the path of a woman seeking an abortion before the fetus attains viability." The meaning of "substantial obstacle" is still being refined fifteen years later.

Casey is important for its contribution to reproductive health law, but it's also an important example of how the Religious Right's fundamentalist attitude toward women seeps into our laws. One of Pennsylvania's restrictions forced married women to sign a statement certifying that they had notified their husbands of the procedure they were about to receive. Fortunately, the Supreme Court determined this was an "undue burden" because it endangered women's lives and well-being and disregarded the "inescapable biological fact" that any antiabortion law has "a far greater impact on the pregnant woman's bodily integrity than it will on the husband."

This case might have turned out the other way if it were decided today because the only lower court judge who supported the spousal-notification provision now has a seat on the nation's highest court. Then U.S. Third Circuit Court of Appeals judge Samuel Alito wrote in dissent that the statute "merely require[d]" a woman to notify her husband, not get his consent. Judge Alito also concluded that the plaintiffs had not demonstrated that the restriction would put women in danger. Not surprisingly, Justice Alito voted to uphold the federal government's ban on "late-term" abortion in the

Supreme Court's latest reproductive health case, *Gonzales v. Carhart,* in 2007. Critics of this decision say that its blatant disregard for women and their health could actually result in banning second-trimester abortions.

The majority also chided the Pennsylvania legislature for perpetuating a fundamentalist view of women. "There was a time, not so long ago," that this restriction wouldn't have been given a second thought, the Court's opinion read. In 1873, for example, "three members of this Court reaffirmed the common law principle that a woman had no legal existence separate from her husband, who was regarded as her head and representative in the social state; and, notwithstanding some recent modifications . . . [this] principle still exist[s] in full force in most States." Today, however, "[A] State may not give to a man the kind of dominion over his wife that parents exercise over their children."

This ringing endorsement of spousal equality enraged the Religious Right. Most conservative Christians believe that the Ephesians 5:22–23 command—"Wives, submit yourselves unto your own husbands as unto the Lord. For the husband is the head of the wife, even as Christ is the head of the church: and he is the savior of the body"—is the only proper marital relationship. Any suggestion that men and women are equal, and should be treated as such, drives them bonkers. Take the word "feminism," for example. Religious Right warhorse Phyllis Schlafly believes it is a "disease" to be "avoided." Now, feminism is neither a medical condition, nor something that can be "avoided" in a free and open society. The dictionary definition is "the theory of the political, economic, and social equality of the sexes." That doesn't make me shake in my boots, but the Religious Right's definition of "feminism" does.

TV preacher Pat Robertson wrote in a fund-raising letter in 1992 that feminism was "not about equal rights for women. It is about a socialist, anti-family political movement that encourages women to leave their husbands, kill their children, practice witchcraft, destroy capitalism, and become lesbians." Who knew? I don't need to belabor the point that the Religious Right doesn't believe women have a right to determine their own futures. As I noted in my speech at the March for Women's Lives in 2004, "They don't think you are moral enough to make your own decisions."

Clearly, the Religious Right has theological objections to comprehensive reproductive health care. For forty years it has fought for laws that reinforce its belief that sex is only for procreation and marital intimacy, not pleasure. Federal, state, and local laws have made it harder for women to get contraception and limited the availability of and access to abortions.

For as "pro-life" and "antiabortion" as the Religious Right claims to be, you would think it would support easy access to birth control. After all, the best way to decrease the abortion rate is to decrease the number of unwanted pregnancies, right? Wrong. Many on the Religious Right are vehemently anti–birth control. They do not believe men and women have the right to have sex for pleasure; sex's only legitimate purpose, they believe, is procreation.

R. Albert Mohler, Jr., president of the Southern Baptist Theological Seminary, believes that birth control ushered in a "contraceptive mentality that sees pregnancy and children as impositions to be avoided rather than gifts to be received, loved and nurtured. This contraceptive mentality is an insidious attack upon God's glory in creation, and the Creator's gift of procreation to the married couple."

Religious conservatives have long been vocal opponents of reproductive rights. Decisions about whether or when to have children are not a woman's, they believe, but her Creator's. Most also believe that a fetus is a "person" who enjoys all the legal rights of a living American from the moment of conception. All abortions, therefore, are tantamount to murder and should be punished accordingly. In their view, many kinds of birth control are also indistinguishable from abortion because many prevent a fertilized egg from implanting in the uterine wall.

A religious fundamentalist mentality is shaping today's reproductive health laws. With help from the Religious Right, conservative politicians have successfully limited access to birth control and abortions in the following ways:

- In 2005, Kansas attorney general Phill Kline subpoenaed medical records from ninety women who had received abortions at clinics in Wichita and Overland Park. His intent was to file criminal charges against the physician for failing to properly report child rape cases and providing late-term abortions. Many accused Kline of abusing his powerful position to push his extreme antiabortion agenda. Kansas voters ousted him from office in November 2006.

- In late 2005, the FDA rebuked a recommendation by its own scientists to offer the "Plan B" emergency contraception pill over the counter. The FDA cited unresolved health concerns for the refusal, but it was under severe pressure from the Religious Right, which was certain the pill would make teen girls more promiscuous.

- In 2006, twenty-nine states enacted sixty-two new laws regulating reproductive health care. The South Dakota legislature became the first in fifteen years to criminalize all abortions unless the woman's life is in danger. The bill passed the legislature with help from the Religious Right, but voters rejected the initiative in November 2006. According to the Guttmacher Institute, a leading reproductive health research organization, the Religious Right is still behind many state efforts to ban all abortions the moment Roe v. Wade is overturned. (It should be noted that if Roe were overturned today, only the states with old anti-choice statutes on the books would immediately ban abortions. The Religious Right would certainly pressure states without these laws to enact them.)

- In 2007, South Carolina moved to require all women seeking abortions to see an ultrasound image of the fetus as a part of mandatory pre-abortion counseling. This strategy, which is strongly supported by religious conservatives, is an effort to deter women from having legal abortions. The Guttmacher Institute reported that, as of early 2007, six states had similar requirements. I think the Religious Right's argument here is that if it looks remotely like a person, then it is a person and therefore protected under the law. (By the way,

*don't try claiming that "person" as a dependent child on your tax
return. You're not going to get very far with that argument when
the IRS comes to your door looking for this child.)*

- Anti-choice religious groups are pressuring states to adopt "conscience clauses" that allow pharmacists and other medical professionals to refuse to provide medications and procedures they say
contradict their religious beliefs. Nine states grant pharmacists the
"right" to refuse to dispense contraception. As of 2007, sixteen conscience clause bills are pending in ten states and the U.S. Congress.

Most people think the right to safe and reliable birth control is
secure. But this right can be eroded, just as the right to legal abortion has been steadily chipped away in recent high court rulings.
While it seeks to overturn *Roe v. Wade* outright, the Religious Right
is more than happy to work on an incremental strategy that seeks
its goals over the long haul. If they win a repeal of that historic ruling, religious conservatives will not stop there. An unprecedented
ability to meddle in the most intimate details of our personal lives
is what these organizations seek.

DEMOCRACY NOT THEOCRACY

> *"Why should we consult attorneys? We have the word of God...
> Principle sometimes takes precedent over silly laws."*
> PASTOR DANIEL LITTLE, Church at Pierce Creek

> *"Well, the way my pastor handled it is, he teaches the values and
> he tells you here's your candidates, and this is what they have
> stated is their belief systems or whatever. You vote, this is what
> we teach."*
> FIRST FREEDOM FIRST Focus Group Member, Albuquerque

Religious leaders frequently speak out on the issues of the day. They
may oppose legal abortion or support it. Some demand gun control,
while others attack it. The list goes on.

Is this robust debate a violation of the separation of church and state? No, it's not. Religious groups, like others, have the right to speak out on the issues. Like other groups, they must expect opposition to the views they express, but their right to speak out is secure.

The right to address issues is protected. But houses of worship have no right to accept tax exemption while endorsing or opposing candidates or intervening in partisan elections.

This distinction—issue advocacy is permitted, intervening in elections is not—has sparked some confusion over the years. It shouldn't. The Internal Revenue Service has, since the 1950s when the tax code was altered, barred nonprofit, 501(c)(3) organizations from intervening in elections. The IRS can do this because tax exemption is a benefit, not a constitutional right. And as a valuable, lucrative benefit, it comes with strings attached. The ability to potentially collect millions in donations every year and pay tax on not even one dime of it is obviously very attractive. One of the conditions that churches, mosques, synagogues, and temples must satisfy for the privilege of not paying taxes (even, for some, on impressive swaths of real estate) is that they not engage in electoral politics. It's not too much to ask.

So why have some still not gotten the message?

Prior to the rise of the Religious Right, this wasn't even an issue in most churches. Most pastors had no interest in telling congregants which candidate to support.

One of the few exceptions was the Christian Echoes National Ministry, founded by Dr. Billy James Hargis in 1951. In 1964, when the ministry endorsed Republican presidential candidate Barry Goldwater, the IRS revoked Christian Echoes' tax-exempt status. The Christian Echoes case is also one of few in which a religious organization actually lost its tax-exempt status; it took an extraordinary action to bring this result.

Some tried to prod the IRS to get more aggressive. In 1980, the group Abortion Rights Mobilization filed suit against the IRS for not taking action against the Roman Catholic Church which, the pro-choice group claimed, had sanctioned open endorsements by its parishes of anti-choice candidates. The suit was dismissed for technical reasons; no ruling was made on its merits.

In the early 1990s, the burgeoning television ministries of evangelists Jimmy Swaggart and Jerry Falwell caught the eye of the IRS, which found, in 1991, that Swaggart had violated the rules governing his ministry's tax-exempt status when he endorsed fellow tel evangelist Pat Robertson for president in 1988. Still, the IRS levied no fine on Swaggart's ministry, nor was his ministry's tax-exempt status affected. The IRS simply made Swaggart promise in writing that he would never violate IRS rules again.

Falwell was not so lucky. In a 1993 IRS investigation, his *Old Time Gospel Hour* was found to have illegally channeled money, during the 1980s, to a political action committee dedicated to supporting right-wing political candidates for office. The *Old Time Gospel Hour* was fined $50,000, and its tax-exempt status was revoked retroactively for the years 1986 and 1987, a fact that Falwell denied to my face during a CNBC interview in 2004. When I showed up at our next face-off—an appearance a few days later on Fox News Channel—with the IRS letter he had signed acknowledging that his group had broken the law, Falwell became visibly agitated.

Despite the financial loss to his television ministry due to its politicking, Falwell seemed not to have learned his lesson. Again, in 1997—the same year in which his television ministry was fined—Falwell's Thomas Road Baptist Church, which he founded and pastored, issued a fax urging churches to "get personally involved" in a GOP primary for attorney general. Falwell lauded the activities of one pastor, who sent a mailing to other Virginia pastors in support of the chosen candidate. As late as 2004, Falwell endorsed, under the auspices of his tax-exempt religious organization, the reelection of President George W. Bush.

It wasn't just the TV preachers. I could not help but notice, when I became executive director of Americans United in 1992, that several pastors hadn't just walked right up to the line when it came to church endorsements—they had leaped right over it.

One case nearly made me spill an entire cup of coffee. I was reading *USA Today* when I saw a full-page ad, paid for by a New York church, that attacked presidential candidate Bill Clinton for his stands on social issues. The '92 Clinton campaign focused on the economy, and the very expensive ad placed by the Church at Pierce Creek led with the headline, "Christians Beware: Do Not Put the Economy Ahead of the Ten Commandments." It blasted Clinton for his stand on social issues and said voting for him was a sin.

At the bottom of the ad, the church included a solicitation for what it called "tax-deductible" donations for the purchase of future advertisements in the same vein! I've seen some pretty brazen material in my day. This was beyond brazen; it was illegal.

In 1995, more than two years after Americans United requested an IRS investigation of the church and its ad-buying program, the Church at Pierce Creek—the home congregation of antiabortion activist and theocrat Randall Terry—lost its tax-exempt status. On the right, the IRS investigation of the Church at Pierce Creek became a cause célèbre, yielding the test case of IRS rules against politicking by churches that the right clearly sought, if not the result delivered by the courts.

Pat Robertson's American Center for Law and Justice (ACLJ) took up the cause, arguing the church had a free speech right to place the ad. It lost. A federal court ruled in favor of the IRS "no-politicking" rules for tax-exempt organizations, a ruling later upheld by a federal appeals court.

During the legal proceedings, the church's pastor, Daniel Little, was defiant. He uttered the words that open this chapter on a now defunct cable television network. Little bragged that he had not sought legal advice before placing the ad. He claimed a religious-freedom right to warn people not to vote for certain candidates.

One would think that religious leaders would have learned a lesson from Little's run-in with "silly laws." And to be fair, most did—or never needed to learn that lesson in the first place. I firmly believe that most religious leaders have no interest in telling their congregants who to vote for or against. They have their hands full attending to spiritual matters and don't see behaving like a political boss as part of their mandate. They know that their congregants come from different political points of view and don't presume to tell some they are right and others they are wrong.

But for the tiny minority who insist on intervening in political races, the case of the Church at Pierce Creek serves as an object lesson. The IRS does enforce this provision. The tax agency does take it seriously.

In fact, every year since the Pierce Creek ruling, the IRS has issued warnings, statements, and reports reminding nonprofit groups not to meddle in elections. The IRS has even launched an entire project, the Political Activity Compliance Initiative, to make sure that the law is being enforced. I point this out because occasionally one hears the claim that the IRS doesn't really enforce the no-politicking rule or is willing to cut churches some slack.

This is wishful thinking. Remember, aside from revocation of tax exemption, there are other steps the IRS can and does take. It can audit a church or require its pastor to sign documents promising to follow the rules from then on.

None of this seems to matter to the Religious Right. Despite its stinging defeat in the Pierce Creek case, the Religious Right was hardly daunted. Instead, the "silencing" of religious voices allegedly represented by the court's ruling became a great fund-raising tool, and legislation was introduced in Congress to repeal the IRS regulations.

Wild allegations were made of pastors being gagged, but this is hardly borne out by the truth. In fact, churches are free to address issues according to the dictates of theology, morality, and conscience. As I noted already, a church may take a stand against legalized abortion, for instance, without invoking the ire of the IRS. It simply can't endorse anti-choice candidates for office.

After the Pierce Creek case, I saw that politicking by religious groups was likely to remain an ongoing problem, so in 1996 Americans United launched Project Fair Play. This special effort is designed to educate religious leaders on the limits of the IRS code, as well as document abuses of tax-exempt status by religious organizations on behalf of candidates on both sides of the political aisle. Since 1996, our organization has submitted sixty-eight complaints to the IRS.

During election years, both Americans United for Separation of Church and State and The Interfaith Alliance often send informational letters to houses of worship nationwide, reminding them that intervention in partisan politics is illegal and that the distribution of biased "voter guides" is considered intervention. We recommend that houses of worship and religious leaders keep all political material produced by outside groups out of the pews.

The project has infuriated the Religious Right. Jay Sekulow, who heads the ACLJ, got so angry one year he convened a press conference and thundered, "The American Center for Law and Justice will meet Mr. Lynn and his organization in every courthouse, in every church, anywhere in the country when he tries to intimidate churches. It's an election season—[Lynn] knows it, we know it. He doesn't have the right to muzzle the church. End of discussion."

Sekulow's patron, Pat Robertson, went even further on his daily television program, *The 700 Club*: "In my humble opinion," Robertson drawled, "anybody who would turn a church in to the IRS is a little bit lower than a child molester." Later in the broadcast, Robertson accused me of "taking the fascist position" of muzzling the speech of religious groups. "In the case of Nazi Germany," Robertson explained, "it was evangelical Christians and Jews. Here, it's apparently evangelical Christians."

AU has not been intimidated by such bluster. Our project, which is evenhanded, examines cases of inappropriate politicking by houses of worship that have backed Republicans, Democrats, and members of other parties. It is not an attempt to muzzle any religious leader's free speech. Indeed, pastors may endorse candidates as private citizens. They simply may not use church resources to promote candidates.

Since the launch of the program, Americans United has documented dozens of incidents of politicking by churches. Here is a sampling:

- *February 2000—At the Allen African Methodist Episcopal Church in Queens, the Rev. Floyd Flake invited Vice President Al Gore to speak, then told congregants, "I don't do endorsements from across the pulpit because I never know who's out there watching the types of laws that govern separation of church and state. But I will say to you this morning and you read it well: this should be the next president of the United States." Flake was visited by IRS agents who asked him to sign documents stating that he would issue no more church endorsements.*

- *November 1996—In Hacienda Heights, California, the Hsi Lai Buddhist Temple actually hosted a Democratic Party fundraiser attended by Vice President Gore.*

- *August 2000—Via satellite from the Greater Exodus Baptist Church in Philadelphia, Pastor Herb Lusk endorsed GOP presidential candidate George W. Bush from his pulpit, while being broadcast to the Republican National Convention, which was taking place in the very same city.*

- *November 2004—The pastor of the East Waynesville Baptist Church in North Carolina endorsed President George W. Bush from the pulpit prior to the November 2004 election. About six months later, he expelled nine Democrats from the church because they voted for John Kerry.*

- *November 2006—The Spirit One Christian Center of Wichita, Kansas, put up marquee signs attacking the Democratic candidates for attorney general and governor.*

- *May 2007—In St. Petersburg, Florida, Bill Keller, in his official capacity as head of Bill Keller Ministries/liveprayer.com, wrote what he called a "devotional" on the ministries' Web site asserting that a vote for GOP presidential candidate Mitt Romney, a Mormon, would be the same as voting for Satan.*

- *August 2007—Former Southern Baptist official and pastor of the First Southern Baptist Church of Buena Park, California, Dr. Wiley Drake, endorsed Republican presidential candidate Mike Huckabee on his church-based radio program. In response to Americans United's complaint to the IRS, Drake issued a press release calling for imprecatory prayer against the organization and several staff members. In a section of his press release called How to Pray, Drake included a long list of biblical citations that call on God to smite enemies. For example, the alleged enemy of God "shall be . . . condemned" and his "days be few." Drake was originally defiant, saying that he would not hesitate to break the tax law again, but stopped talking to the press on advice of his lawyers shortly thereafter.*

I am often asked why Americans United continues to compile examples of improper involvement in politics by religious bodies. There are two answers to that. One is that church politicking on behalf of or in opposition to a candidate is illegal. The overwhelming majority of secular nonprofit groups in America are willing and able to abide by this rule. Houses of worship should not expect special treatment.

The second reason is perhaps more subtle but equally compelling: pulpit politicking is bad for the church and the government. This type of political deal smacks of unhealthy tit for tat: "You endorse me, and I give you . . . what?" Religious leaders should not behave like lobbyists for the tobacco industry, agribusiness, or defense contractors. They should not play these games. Their arguments should be based on moral suasion and the respect for faith that is common in American public life. Religious leaders should never be in the position of asking, "If I endorse you, Senator Jones, what's in it for me? What do I get in return?"

And let's be honest; it's the politician who will benefit here. A religious leader may think he's savvy enough to outfox a professional politician, but the reality is that when church and state relate in this way, it's usually the preacher who comes out looking bad. Congregants will want to know why the pulpit has been prostituted for a perceived political gain—a gain that may very well prove to be illusory.

In short, when a religious leader looks to a politician for salvation, well, in my view, at least, he's putting his faith in a mere mortal above his faith in the eternal.

ACADEMIC INTEGRITY

> *"I hope I will live to see the day when, as in the early days of our country, we won't have any public schools. The churches will have taken them over again and Christians will be running them. What a happy day that will be!"*
> JERRY FALWELL, 1979

I have previously discussed some of the important legal cases involving prohibitions against teaching evolution or forced inclusion of information about creationism or intelligent design. Aside from obvious issues of the separation of church and state, teaching non-science as science raises fundamental questions of academic integrity. We should demand that our children be given an education based on the best available evidence and on standards set by scholars and professionals.

When I encounter visitors from abroad, they often ask me why the United States is still having fights over the teaching of evolution. In part, it is because we don't have a very good grasp of what science is, nor do we have any systematic way—other than the mass media—to let citizens know about new scientific developments in any field. Moreover, powerful fundamentalist groups have developed a sophisticated propaganda arm that attacks the credibility of evolution—a concept they wrongly insist presents some threat to the survival of faith in this country.

Because public education in America is decentralized, battles over the teaching of evolution can erupt just about anywhere. Occasionally, people are elected to school boards on a platform of fiscal discipline that sounds reasonable; then, once seated, they begin pursuing a fundamentalist religious agenda. Evolution is normally the first thing that ends up in the crosshairs.

I've seen this happen time and time again. In the 1990s, a veritable spate of these battles erupted from coast to coast. The script was familiar: a board majority under the sway of some Religious Right outfit would seek to either introduce creationism outright or water down the instruction of evolution. On occasion, these boards would promote the use of "supplemental" materials produced by creationist outfits. This was all done in the guise of "offering alternatives" or "encouraging debate."

Of course, real debate was the last thing these people wanted. In a real debate featuring actual scientists, creationism is exposed for the nonscience that it is. What these boards wanted was to bring a fundamentalist interpretation of the Bible into the public schools dressed in an ill-fitting lab coat. It did not work.

Voters usually rebelled and sent the fundamentalists packing after the next election. Frustrated, advocates of creationism took their idea back to the drawing board and emerged for the umpteenth time with a retooled version. This time they called it intelligent design.

Known as ID for short, intelligent design is perhaps misnamed, as there is little intelligent about it. ID jettisons the more outlandish claims of the old-style creationists—the six-thousand-year-old Earth, the dinosaurs basking under the sun while cruising on Noah's Ark—and substitutes instead the claim that human beings are pretty complex things, therefore they must have been designed. Who or what did the designing? ID advocates won't call it God (except when speaking before what they believe are friendly audiences) and actually do posit the possibility of space aliens or even time travelers from another dimension.

Stripped down and lean, ID remains the same warmed-over exercise in evolution bashing that was not persuasive thirty years ago. Its advocates like to nitpick at supposed "gaps" in evolution. Then, when a gap, say, in the fossil record, is filled by the discovery of a new fossil—call it species C somewhere between A and F—ID advocates say: "There's still a gap between A and C!" They complain that evolution is "just a theory," likening scientific theory to a hunch or an unsubstantiated guess. However, a scientific theory is not just a guess. According to the National Center for Science Education, a "scientific theory" is a "logical, tested [and] well-supported explanation" for a variety of observable phenomena. True, theories are not "facts," but some have so much supportive evidence that they come pretty close. In this regard, evolution is right up there with the theories of gravity and electromagnetism.

The grand overlay to this attack is to argue that human beings, and indeed the whole of creation, are filled with such complex assemblages that nothing but a designer of some kind could possibly have generated this state of affairs. This may sound familiar. Thomas Aquinas employed an "argument from design" in the eleventh century. More recently, William Paley in the nineteenth century used it to "prove" the existence of God.

Intelligent design generated a huge media buzz in 1999 when a majority of the Kansas state school board insisted that the curriculum must include discussion of intelligent design. The state soon became a national laughingstock and the Republican governor was so incensed that he threatened to dissolve the entire school board. A number of major science and biotechnology corporations hinted that they might not locate new businesses in the state out of fear of scientific illiteracy.

The state fought over the matter for years, with the board seesawing back and forth four times between proponents of ID and evolution backers. As of this writing, the evolutionists have the upper hand. Ohio had a similar though less lengthy spat over the issue. It ended with the IDers in retreat—for now. (Like ants at a picnic, they never truly go away.)

I mentioned earlier a case called *Kitzmiller v. Dover Area School District*. Creationists soldier on despite these losses and are nothing if not, well, creative. They continue to stress discredited arguments to undermine the teaching of evolution. First, some are arguing that teachers have an "academic freedom" right to teach what they think is appropriate in a classroom. This kind of argument is nothing new and has been rejected by courts consistently. It is an erroneous interpretation of the academic freedom doctrine. The American Association of University Professors (AAUP) defines academic freedom as the ability of a given discipline's qualified scholars to establish and interpret scholarship standards in their respective academic profession. The AAUP is adamant that academic freedom is not a carte blanche for teachers, especially public school teachers, to "introduce into their teaching controversial matter which has no relation to their subject." Indeed, the AAUP goes on to say that while one of academic freedom's principal goals is to "foster a plurality of methodologies and perspectives," it does not require teachers or academic institutions to yield to philosophies "not deemed a reasonable scholarly option within the discipline."

The second argument is that schools should "teach the controversy." The argument is that there is a battle about evolution going on, and students should be taught all sides. Unfortunately for creationists, the battle is all in their minds. Real scientists are not arguing about the reality of evolution any more than they are questioning whether the sun is the center of the solar system. Of course there are some real controversies related to evolution—but whether or not it occurs is not one of them.

In this arena, we see the Right's strong effort to force the inclusion of nonscientific information into a science curriculum. Ironically, in the context of one other form of public school education, however, the Right argues precisely that just because it may be scientifically valid doesn't mean you should teach it. The topic I'm thinking about is human sexuality.

In 1996, as part of a much-debated package of changes in federal welfare laws, a conservative Congress added a line of funding for states for "abstinence only before marriage" sex education programs. It is a $50 million per year mandatory spending program (with an additional $37.5 million in matching funds for states) that targets teenagers with the message that the only way to prevent pregnancy and contracting of sexually transmitted disease is through sexual abstinence. No discussion of artificial contraception is permitted—even if the discussion includes young people who are already sexually active.

There are no peer-reviewed studies that indicate that these programs work to lead people to remain abstinent until marriage. A few studies do seem to indicate that for some groups there can be a slight delay in first sexual activity. The bad news, though, is that those young people tend to engage in the riskiest forms of sexual intercourse. This is because they are unaware of other forms of sexual expression and unfamiliar with the use of birth control methods. Their ignorance, generated by government policy, can spawn undesirable social consequences and can even be fatal. Remember, too, that if states want to get the government funding, they must match it with state funds, which as a practical matter nearly always means taking funds from their previously used comprehensive, age-appropriate sex education initiatives.

The most recent study as of this writing was accurately summarized by *Congressional Quarterly:* "The study concluded that students given abstinence education were no more likely to abstain from sex, that those who had sex did so with a similar number of partners as those who did not receive abstinence education and that those students first had sex at the same mean age."

I happen to believe that most young people (and plenty of older persons) are not well served by sexual activity outside of a committed relationship. However, being in touch with today's reality, I know that a significant percentage of them will. The Religious Right thinks in more dire terms about this, but many Americans find it hard to believe that the Right doesn't at least want to "protect" those young people who are making decisions it doesn't approve of from dire health consequences. An explanation for part of this is, frankly, economic. For example, a high percentage of books and other materials used in these abstinence-only curricula are written by ministers or others connected with Christian-based advocacy groups. They like the corner they have on that marketplace.

Lately, a new factor has entered the equation. All totaled, it looks like the federal government has now spent in excess of half a billion dollars on these programs, all doled out to groups that promise never to mention a condom. These tend to be religiously oriented groups of the conservative theological persuasion. A lawsuit was filed in 2002 by the ACLU of Louisiana alleging that the governor was defying a court order not to fund religious activities, messages, or instruction through abstinence-only education legislation. As of 2005, the federal court in Louisiana had refused to hold the governor in contempt for "continuing to preach with taxpayer dollars." Also in 2005, the American Civil Liberties Union of Massachusetts filed a lawsuit against government funding of the "Silver Ring Thing"; it is the only successfully completed lawsuit to date.

According to legal papers filed by the ACLU of Massachusetts, the Silver Ring Thing describes its mission as "offering a personal relationship with Jesus Christ as the best way to live a sexually pure life." Silver Ring Thing participants testified about how accepting Jesus Christ improved their lives, quoted Bible passages, and urged audience members to ask the Lord Jesus Christ to come into their lives.

The silver ring in question, which participants can purchase for $15, is inscribed with a biblical verse from 1 Thessalonians 4:3–4: "God wants you to be holy, so you should keep clear of all sexual sin. Then each of you will control your body and live in holiness and honor."

No one is suggesting that people in the United States have to agree about matters of human sexuality. However, when overtly sectarian viewpoints are being funded (to the exclusion of all others), it undercuts the principle of separation of church and state and leads to education that lacks the integrity of encompassing the best information on all the topics of the curriculum in a public school or other venue in which government-funded activities may be occurring.

A final area where academic integrity is threatened is censorship. This is a sprawling topic, and it can only be touched on briefly here. Suffice it to say that no one should make the mistake of thinking that because we have a First Amendment in our Constitution, we have no censorship. We have plenty of it.

Most battles revolve around (surprise!) the public schools. From *Of Mice and Men* to *The Catcher in the Rye,* literature aimed at young people is always suspect to self-appointed moral guardians.

Most recent offerings have only driven the Religious Right into a more intense fury. J. K. Rowling's phenomenally popular series of books about boy wizard Harry Potter are frequently attacked for promoting witchcraft. Apparently, no one in the Religious Right ever read the Brothers Grimm or they'd know that this fictional material about "witches" has been around for quite a while. Real Wiccans may not appreciate this imagery, but they aren't trying to ban it from America's schools.

Most public schools will make an accommodation if a parent really does not like a novel that has been assigned. That is never enough for the censors. They want everyone to lose access to the book they find offensive. Laura Mallory, a Georgia woman who obviously has too much time on her hands, has waged a relentless crusade to ban the Potter books in Gwinnett County's schools. School officials have heard her out several times but voted to keep the books. One school official noted that if Mallory had her way, Shakespeare's *Macbeth* could be next for the trash heap.

It's not only our schools that face these threats. We should never assume that our public libraries are safe from censorship. Over the years, Religious Right groups have come up with plans to "help" parents by pressuring libraries to put certain material on restricted access or cordon it off in special rooms. Not surprisingly, the material they want to make harder to get centers on topics like human sexuality, the "occult" (a term they define very broadly), or criticism of religion.

Responsible parents don't need the Religious Right's assistance. They are capable of accompanying their children to the library and helping them make appropriate choices. For all of its talk about "pro-family" policies, it often seems that the Religious Right is unwilling to let families make their own decisions.

As a minister, I know that there was a time when some misguided members of the clergy attacked more or less all forms of literature. Reading novels was a waste of time, they asserted. You should be scrutinizing the Bible instead. I'd like to think we've moved beyond that now. Indeed, lots of great literature alludes to the Bible—where do you think John Steinbeck got the title for *East of Eden?*—and we strive to teach our children that it's just fun to read in its own right.

I hate to believe that any force in our society willfully fosters ignorance, but I've listened to so many fundamentalists over the years making baseless accusations against books they clearly have not read that I can only conclude that some people do prefer to remain in the dark. They have the right to cower in there. They don't have the right to drag other people's children in with them. Stopping them is essential to preserving American schools' academic integrity.

SOUND SCIENCE

> *"Human embryonic stem cell research represents a barbaric assault on the dignity of humankind."*
>
> SOUTHERN BAPTIST CONVENTION STATEMENT
> ON HUMAN STEM CELL RESEARCH, October 2004

Once upon a time, facts were something that mattered. But since the ascendancy of the Religious Right into the inner reaches of the White House, facts have become less important than faith and ideology. It's not just any faith that matters, of course, but born-again, Christian, and often fundamentalist faith. As for facts, not only do they take a back seat to faith, but if they are seen as threatening to Religious Right doctrine, they are often thrown over the side of the ship of state.

In 2004, author Ron Suskind published a profile of President Bush's White House in the *New York Times Magazine* that detailed the president's faith-based, messianic sense of mission, and his rejection of doubt. When Suskind met with a senior aide to Bush, the aide criticized the journalist as being a member "of the reality-based community" who "believe[s] that solutions emerge from your judicious study of discernible reality... That's not the way the world really works anymore."

As Americans, one of our great boasts has been our skill at advancing technology. From the first sound recording to the first iPod, from advanced medical care to the space program, we have all but taken for granted our nation's ability to apply scientific discovery to real-life uses. But if we continue down the path on which we currently find ourselves, I fear we will become a society in which advances take a back seat to ignorance perpetuated by the state in the name of God. It's a dire claim, I know. But consider two recent developments:

- *Federal policy on climate change has been altered because of a theologically based rejection of the urgency with which most climate scientists believe that global warming—the result of an increase in greenhouse gases primarily due to human activity—needs to be addressed. The Religious Right seems split over the issue of climate change. The most prominent faction labels the whole thing a myth, a plot cooked up by globalists at the United Nations for some nefarious purpose (perhaps to usher in one-world government, a long-standing UN goal according to this fringe). Others accept climate change but argue that human activity has nothing to do with it and assert that little to nothing can be done about it. A third faction, perhaps the most extreme, basically says global warming does not matter because Jesus will be coming back soon. God gave us the planet, and by gum, we have the right to run it into the ground. A number of Religious Right leaders embrace climate change as a sign of an imminent Rapture and the subsequent return of Jesus Christ.*

- *Federal funding for medical research into a range of potential therapies for such devastating diseases as Alzheimer's and Parkinson's has been curtailed because the work at present requires embryonic stem cells. These are easily acquired from the unused embryos created in the in vitro fertilization process, but politically problematic because of the theological views of an influential constituency of one political party. The Religious Right equates the use of embryonic stem cells with murder. Hence, these groups have sought to curtail tax funding of further research in this area no matter who it might benefit—even over the protests of a few notable conservatives such as Nancy Reagan.*

Let's look at these issues in a little more detail.

The Religious Right's effort to deny climate change is rapidly taking its place alongside creationism as the far right's greatest pseudoscience. Religious Right leaders like James Dobson, Tony Perkins, Pat Robertson, and the late Jerry Falwell—all of whom have attacked global warming in some form or another—are not climatologists. They are not meteorologists. They are not even television weather forecasters. Yet they assure us we need not fear climate change or they deny that it is happening altogether.

Like the 150-year-old discovery of evolution, the evidence of climate change resulting from human activity is rejected as hogwash. Senator James Inhofe (R-OK), who has a nearly 100 percent rating from the Christian Coalition, famously called global warming "the greatest hoax ever perpetrated on the American people."

Opposition to measures that would curtail the emission of greenhouse gasses remains the rule among the older, more established leaders of the Religious Right, some of whose rejection of such measures stems from theological roots. They see global warming as evidence that the Rapture is at hand—the moment before the Apocalypse when the faithful followers of Jesus Christ will be swept up to heaven before the Great Tribulation of war, pestilence, disease, and famine that will precede the returning Christ's thousand-year reign on earth. Known as dispensationalism, this is what leaders such as Pat Robertson speak to when they see God's retribution for a sinful world in every natural disaster and act of terrorism.

Prior to the 2006 congressional elections, this was actually the view that held sway in Congress. Former House majority leader Tom DeLay based his opposition to global warming mitigation measures on the teachings of Rev. John Hagee of Texas, who has cheerfully declared the war in Iraq to be the "gateway to Apocalypse," words that DeLay branded as "the truth from God." DeLay counts himself among the 20 million or so Christian Zionists who believe the creation of the state of Israel in 1948 to be the beginning of the end of the world as we know it. In DeLay's Capitol Hill office hung a sign referring to Judgment Day, according to his biographers Jan Reid and Lou Dubose, that read: "Today could be the day."

This explains why far-right Christian crusaders spend so much time obsessing over this issue. As much as I disagree with the Religious Right on issues like reproductive choice, I can at least understand their interest in it. There is a moral dimension. But climate change involves no fetuses, no prayers, no alleged violations of religious exercise. So why the vociferous opposition? It appears some of them may actually believe that God gave the planet to humankind, and we have the right to destroy it if we're so inclined. It's a chilling thought, but not so much that it takes the edge off the obvious reality of drowning polar bears, melting glaciers, and formerly snow-capped mountain peaks now showing bare ground most of the year.

The only other thing I can figure out is that protecting the environment is often perceived as a "leftist" issue; therefore, it must be opposed in knee-jerk fashion by the Religious Right. Leaders of the Religious Right take this issue seriously. Woe to anyone who dares suggest their ideas are not only ignorant but dangerous. And special woe to any conservative Christian who dares suggest that God did indeed give us the planet—and fully expects us to care for it.

Conservative Christians generally do a pretty good job of maintaining a unified front, despite rivalries and differences in style or on finer theological points. But occasionally an issue comes to the fore that exposes cracks in the alliance between right-wing Christian evangelists, as has climate change.

Opposition to legislation or global agreements that aim to limit the amount of greenhouse gases emitted by cars and buildings in the U.S. is usually based on an argument similar to that advanced by creationists: accepted scientific realities are rejected as mere hypothetical "theories," despite the mountains of evidence that exist to support them.

The view that global warming is not a problem is advanced by the Interfaith Council for Environmental Stewardship, which, according to journalist Glenn Scherer, is "a radical-right Christian organization founded by radio evangelist James Dobson, dispensationalist Rev. D. James Kennedy of Coral Ridge Ministries, Jerry Falwell, and Robert Sirico, a Catholic priest..."

The Council was formed because some evangelicals dared to suggest that it's time to take climate change seriously. This group spoke not of humankind's "dominion" over the earth but rather our "stewardship" of the planet, implying a mandate to protect the earth and creation from harm.

Similarly, in 2004, members of the Evangelical Environmental Network launched the "What Would Jesus Drive?" campaign, a clever twist on a guiding question evangelicals are taught to ask of themselves when facing difficult choices: what would Jesus do? The campaign was designed to drive support for a bill that would have regulated greenhouse gas emissions and instituted a scheme of "carbon credits" (as well as prod people to rethink the wisdom of motoring around in large, gas-guzzling SUVs).

Taking the lead in evangelical environmentalism was Rev. Rick Cizik, vice president of governmental affairs for the National Association of Evangelicals, who recently took a thumping from the old-guard leaders of the Religious Right.

At the outset of the evangelical green movement, it appeared as though some accommodation between the new green crowd and the elders might take shape. Many joined together to sign a statement in 2005, titled "Evangelical Call to Civic Responsibility," that read in part, "Because clean air, pure water, and adequate resources are crucial to public health and civic order, government has an obligation to protect its citizens from the effects of environmental degradation." Signatories included Dobson and Chuck Colson, the Watergate-era figure who runs Prison Fellowship Ministries.

Two years later, however, Cizik came under fire from Dobson, Perkins, former Family Research Council president Gary Bauer, and Paul Weyrich, cofounder of the Heritage Foundation and one of the Religious Right's chief strategists. In the spring of 2007, the group sent a letter to the National Association of Evangelicals demanding that Cizik stop speaking out on global warming. According to the *New York Times*, the letter said, "We have observed that Cizik and others are using the global warming controversy to shift the emphasis away from the great moral issues of our time." Those issues, the letter went on to say, are abortion and homosexuality, among others.

The National Association of Evangelicals, to its credit, pointed out that none of the people who signed the letter belong to the National Association of Evangelicals. It declined to fire Cizik.

Global warming is an example of an issue where the Religious Right does not like what science says, so it substitutes pseudo science instead. The controversy over stem cell research is a bit different. Here the Religious Right argues that theology must actually trump science, even if the science in question holds great promise in curing debilitating diseases.

Disputes like this are often portrayed by the Religious Right as a clash of worldviews: a faith-based approach versus one of cold scientific rationality. In fact, this is not an apt comparison. Science is not a worldview; it is a process. It is a way of discovering truth, open to change and constantly adapting to new information.

Religion, especially the fundamentalist variety, can be stubbornly resistant to change. Fundamentalism insists that the answers to all questions, even those of a scientific nature, are found in the Bible or some other sacred text. (This is a curious assertion, given that the Bible nowhere claims to be a science text. Indeed, it was written in a prescientific era.)

Science, to be effective, cannot be subservient to any ideology, including a religious one. The Religious Right seeks science that bows to its interpretation of its holy text. When advanced technologies hold out the promise of mitigating the ravages of such devastating diseases as Alzheimer's and Parkinson's, the Religious Right leadership wants to impose its theology to say, "Not allowed."

In 1995, in response to a recommendation from the National Institutes of Health that federal funding be made available for research on human embryos left over from in vitro fertilization procedures, Congress passed a law that forbade federal funding for research that resulted in the destruction of an embryo.

In 1998, scientists discovered that certain cells from human embryos were capable of growing into any of a number of organs. Less than three years later, researchers at the University of Wisconsin and Johns Hopkins found a way to isolate and culture the embryonic stem cells. For patients suffering from diseases arising from the deterioration of organs or systems, the use of stem cells in research offers the means by which the processes of cell generation may suggest new, restorative therapies. But the Religious Right will not hear of it.

Because the research depends on the use of stem cells from human embryos—a supply of which languishes in fertility clinics as a result of the process by which in vitro fertilization is done—Religious Right leaders harnessed their theological view that human life begins at the moment that sperm meets egg to oppose federal funding for embryonic stem cell research. (Indeed, the creation of more human embryos than are generally used for an in vitro fertilization procedure accounts for the opposition of the Roman Catholic Church to most of the new fertilization technologies.)

Even after President Bill Clinton signed the law known as the Dickey Amendment that Congress passed barring federal funding for research involving the destruction of human embryos, his administration interpreted the law in such a way that embryonic stem cell research was funded in a limited way. Once George W. Bush took office, that changed. After August 2001, federal funding could only be granted for research on already existing lines of human embryos—a limited pool of sixty lines, some of which have proven useless because of contamination.

During the 2006 debate over opening up new sources, White House spokesman Tony Snow said the president would veto any such bill because, "The simple answer is he thinks murder's wrong." (Snow later backpedaled, denying that Bush would use the term "murder." He added, "I think there's concern. The president has said that he believes that this is the destruction of human life.")

It's important to note here that in vitro fertilization is legal in the United States, as are birth control and certain types of abortion. Opposition to stem cell research, like nearly all opposition to abortion and birth control, is theological in nature. Dire warnings about the creation of human clones for research amount to fearmongering; diligent government regulation can stave off such violations of medical ethics.

While Religious Right leaders cast embryonic stem cell research as the destruction of human life for nefarious purposes, the real threat the research poses may be to the movement's attempt to debunk the theory of evolution. Through the study of embryonic stem cells, scientists get to view a segment of the evolutionary process in grand detail. And if the evolutionary process can be harnessed to save lives, it's quite likely to earn good reviews among the general public, which in turn might embrace government support for the teaching of science. For the Religious Right, that would be a tragedy indeed.

NO RELIGIOUS DISCRIMINATION

"Our civil rights have no dependence on our religious opinions . . . therefore the proscribing any citizen as unworthy the public confidence by laying upon him an incapacity of being called to the offices of trust and emolument, unless he profess or renounce this or that religious opinion, is depriving him injuriously of those privileges and advantages to which in common with his fellow citizens he has a natural right."

THE VIRGINIA ACT FOR ESTABLISHING
RELIGIOUS FREEDOM, 1786

"No one can legitimately challenge the fact that the God America refers to in the Pledge, our national motto, and other places is the monotheistic God of the Jewish and Christian faith. There is no historic connection between America and the polytheistic creed of the Hindu faith. I seriously doubt that Americans want to change the motto, 'In God We Trust' . . . to 'In gods we trust.' [By allowing a Hindu to offer the opening prayer,] that is essentially what the United States Senate did today."

TONY PERKINS, July 12, 2007

Religious discrimination is not a new problem in the United States. Contrary to what many of us were taught in grade school, the Puritans who fled religious persecution in Europe did not support religious liberty as we understand it today. They supported their *own* religious freedom, but expelled, tortured, and even occasionally executed their detractors.

Religious persecution gradually diffused into toleration and then into equality as America's unique church-state separation model took shape. The ratification of Article VI's "no religious test" clause in 1789, the First Amendment's religion clauses in 1791, the Fourteenth Amendment's Equal Protection Clause in 1868, and statutes passed to enforce it eventually banned overt government-initiated discrimination in this country.

As early as 1790, President George Washington lauded his countrymen for their commitment to religious equality. In a letter that year to Newport, Rhode Island's, Touro Synagogue, he wrote, "It is now no more that toleration is spoken of, as if it was by the indulgence of one class of people, that another enjoyed the exercise of their inherent national gifts." Sadly, these legal reforms did not wash away political and religious majorities' disdain toward religious minorities. As we'll discover in this chapter, and also later in the discussion on the right to "Worship . . . Or Not," government-sponsored religious discrimination is still a problem in the United States.

Perhaps you're wondering why I only mentioned "government-initiated" religious discrimination. Isn't *all* religious discrimination a problem, you ask? Well, yes, it can be, but it is not my intent to make that case here. In fact, there is one instance when religious discrimination is legally acceptable. Title VII of the 1964 Civil Rights Act generally prohibits employers from discriminating on the basis of race, color, religion, sex, or national origin when hiring or firing employees. Religious institutions are exempt from Title VII because maintaining a single-faith staff is crucial to defining and executing such an organization's mission. Obviously, a synagogue must have the right to turn away a Muslim or atheist who applies to be a rabbi or religious education teacher. Religious organizations have wide latitude in determining whom they employ; indeed, they may even discriminate when hiring for nonreligious jobs.

The U.S. Supreme Court considered whether extending the Title VII religious exemption to secular jobs was constitutional in *Corporation of Presiding Bishop v. Amos*. The Court ruled unanimously in 1987 that a religious organization can indeed discriminate in any privately funded position. *Amos* involved Frank Mayson, a janitor at The Church of Jesus Christ of Latter-day Saints Desert Gymnasium in Salt Lake City, Utah. Mayson had worked at the gym for sixteen years but was fired after he failed to produce a "temple recommend," or a certificate that he was a member in good standing with the Mormon Church. Mayson challenged the church's decision under Title VII of the Civil Rights Act following his termination. He argued that, while the Church was exempt from the antidiscrimination law when filling ecclesiastical positions, Title VII and the Establishment Clause forbade discrimination in secular positions like his. The Court disagreed, holding that religious organizations are permitted to discriminate when filling any privately funded internal position.

It is difficult for many of us to accept the idea that religious organizations can discriminate based on religious affiliation or "moral conduct." (Courts have held that Catholic schools can fire unwed pregnant teachers because premarital sex is against the Catholic doctrine). My concern, however, is that many politicians want to let them discriminate when hiring for jobs we as taxpayers are funding. We'll explore this problem in the next section. For now, I want to reiterate that the government must treat all religious and nonreligious people and institutions equally, and explain why the federal and some state and local governments aren't living up to that basic responsibility.

Much of this problem revolves around so-called faith-based initiatives. These initiatives have been around in one form or another for more than a decade, but as I noted earlier, they took off in earnest when President Bush entered office in 2001. The initiatives were to be one of his defining domestic policy accomplishments. I think the only thing they have accomplished is injuring our nation's healthy separation between church and state. Recall that Congress never approved a bill authorizing these programs; President Bush created them via executive order in early 2001 and uses annual "discretionary funds" to implement them. Although comprehensive data do not exist, it is estimated that billions of dollars have been spent on the initiatives during the course of Bush's administration.

Faith-based initiatives may violate the Establishment Clause in three major ways: First, they force taxpayers to subsidize religious organizations. Justice Hugo Black wrote in *Everson v. Board of Education* that one of the Establishment Clause's basic purposes is to ensure that "No tax in any amount, large or small, can be levied to support any religious activities or institutions, whatever they may be called or whatever form they may adopt to teach or practice religion." I believe that funding faith-based initiatives is no different from forcing taxpayers to put money in the collection plates of churches, synagogues, temples, and mosques.

Second, the few safeguards meant to ensure that public funds are not used for religious purposes are wholly inadequate. The order says grantees must separate religious activities from secular activities and only bill the government for the latter. This may be an insurmountable hurdle to overcome, even if there were adequate government oversight and bookkeeping assistance. As I discussed in the earlier section on aid to religious schools, religious organizations are inherently religious; they cannot possibly separate their religious identity from their activities. I don't think religious organizations should be asked to abandon their identities when providing social services, but taxpayers must not foot the bill. In the pre-Bush era, religious groups that received government funds (e.g., Lutheran Child Services and Catholic Charities) presumably did not proselytize in publicly funded programs.

Finally, faith-based initiatives permit taxpayer-funded religious discrimination. According to the Bush administration's interpretation of current law, a fundamentalist Christian group that receives public funds to staff secular social service positions can hang up a sign that says "Jews and Catholics Need Not Apply." That's not "compassionate conservatism," that's outrageous bigotry!

Our founders would be troubled by our digression because they believed religious bigotry in government had come and gone by the late eighteenth century. President George Washington concluded his letter to the Touro Synagogue by writing that the U.S. Government "gives to bigotry no sanction, to persecution no assistance" and believes that the only measure of a citizen is his or her contribution to society. Now we are trying to give the bigots and persecutors of which he spoke social service grants!

Part of my objection to faith-based initiatives is that religious organizations are the only groups exempt from antidiscrimination laws. Secular groups that receive faith-based initiative funds still have to follow the law. Not only are these religious groups getting special treatment, they're using our money to discriminate, potentially against us! Say for example, a religious group receives funds to operate a soup kitchen. You want to help feed the hungry, so you apply for a staff position at this soup kitchen. Unfortunately for you, you aren't the same faith as the sponsoring organization, so you don't get the job. It doesn't matter that you're an excellent soup server, you care about the cause, and your tax dollars help pay for the soup; you are not worthy to work because you do not share the organization's religious beliefs.

Faith-based funds are powerful recruiting tools for religious groups that administer social service programs in underserved communities. Faith-based social services are especially popular in prisons because many religious groups believe inmates can be rehabilitated through faith. Having taxpayers pay for religious conversion raises serious constitutional concerns.

In 2003, Americans United challenged such a program at the Newton Iowa Correctional Facility. The program, InnerChange Freedom Initiative (IFI), is an arm of Watergate figure Charles Colson's Prison Fellowship Ministries (PFM). As its name implies, IFI's mission is to transform prisoners through "biblical teaching that stresses . . . the reality of a new life in Christ." We challenged the financial relationship between the state of Iowa and PFM because we believed taxpayers' funding of IFI's pervasively sectarian programming and discriminatory practices violated the Establishment Clause.

The Ministry insisted that it would only use public funds for "secular," not religious, parts of the program. It was an odd claim, since IFI appeared to be a full-time Christian boot camp. To illustrate this problem, I'd like to focus on the taxpayer-funded religious discrimination that permeated the IFI program at the Newton Correctional Facility.

All IFI employees and volunteers were required to sign a statement of faith. It was explicit, not only saying that the applicant would support the organization's mission, but laying out a number of doctrinal teachings the applicant had to profess in order to get the supposedly secular, taxpayer-funded job. For example, prospective employees and volunteers had to affirm that they believed "in one God, Creator and Lord of the Universe; the coeternal Trinity: Father, Son, and Holy Spirit," that the Bible is "without error in all its teachings," that "all people are lost sinners and cannot see the Kingdom of Heaven except through the new birth," and that as born-again Christians, they had an obligation to "save" (i.e., convert) these "lost sinners."

Not surprisingly, IFI's religious perspective manifested itself in employees' interaction with inmates. Testimony from our fourteen-day trial revealed "constant tension" between staff and nonevangelical Christian inmates. For example, one Roman Catholic participant said a staff member "compared the pope to Hitler and the Antichrist" and wouldn't let him attend mass. A Native American inmate was confronted by an IFI employee and told that his spiritual practices were "witchcraft, against the Bible, sorcery, and worship of false idols." The inmate was discharged from the program for "not growing spiritually" and not fully participating in revival services.

In June 2006, Federal District Court judge Robert Pratt ruled that Iowa and PFM's financial contract violated the Establishment Clause on a number of grounds. First and foremost, it unconstitutionally advanced religion by providing direct grants to a pervasively sectarian program that was unable to separate its secular and religious aspects. "For all practical purposes," Pratt wrote, "the state has literally established an Evangelical Christian congregation within the walls of one of its penal institutions, giving the leaders of that congregation, i.e., InnerChange employees, authority to control the spiritual, emotional, and physical lives of hundreds of Iowa inmates." Furthermore, "There are no adequate safeguards present, nor could there be to ensure that state funds are not being directly spent to indoctrinate Iowa inmates."

Second, IFI lacked the neutrality and "true private choice" Justice Sandra Day O'Connor stressed in the 2002 school voucher case, *Zelman v. Simmons-Harris.* Justice O'Connor had made clear in her concurring opinion that any publicly funded program must be administered in a "neutral fashion, without differentiation based on the religious status of beneficiaries or providers of services" and program participants must have "a genuine choice among religious and nonreligious organizations." "If the answer to either query is 'no,'" she concluded, "the program should be struck down under the Establishment Clause."

Judge Pratt concluded that the contract met neither requirement and that PFM's "assertion that all inmates are welcome in the program is true in form only. In practice," he continued, "the intensive religious content of the InnerChange program is a substantial disincentive to joining for persons of other faiths, or those professing no faith. . . . The contractual relationship between the state and InnerChange does not make the treatment program here available, in practice, to a 'broad class of individual recipients defined without regard to religion.'" Finally, Judge Pratt concluded that the financial relationship between Iowa and IFI, which necessitates considerable government oversight, unconstitutionally "fosters excessive entanglement between the state and religion."

Prison Fellowship Ministries appealed the decision and a three-judge panel (including former justice O'Connor) of the Eighth U.S. Circuit Court of Appeals heard arguments in November 2006. We were awaiting that court's decision as this book went to press.

Amos dealt with religious discrimination in privately funded secular jobs. The U.S. Supreme Court has not yet considered whether religious organizations retain their Title VII exemption when hiring for publicly funded secular jobs, like those financed by many faith-based initiatives. Only a handful of federal courts have taken up the issue. One ruled that religious organizations do not have the right to discriminate in publicly funded secular jobs, others ruled that they do have that right, and another recently approved a settlement deal directing a religious organization not to discriminate in hiring for publicly funded positions. A 1989 district court case from Mississippi, *Dodge v. Salvation Army,* was the first to consider Title VII exemptions for publicly funded jobs inside religious organizations. Jamie Dodge was a victims' assistance coordinator with a Salvation Army–operated domestic violence shelter. She was fired from that position when her employer discovered that she was a practicing Wiccan. She sued, alleging that the organization had no right to fire her from the publicly funded job based on her religion. The court agreed with Ms. Dodge, ruling that the Salvation Army's contract with the government, in this instance, compelled it to follow federal antidiscrimination laws.

In the second case, *Lown v. Salvation Army,* a group of current and former social workers in a program operated by the Salvation Army brought suit alleging New York City had, among other things, unconstitutionally used public funds to finance discriminatory hiring practices. The plaintiffs made a very convincing argument that the Salvation Army should not be allowed to discriminate based on religion when hiring for publicly funded secular jobs. The Salvation Army, plaintiffs argued, was providing a service on behalf of the state and should not mix religion with their secular services.

Unfortunately, Federal District Court judge Sidney Stein dismissed the plaintiffs' claims on September 30, 2006. Judge Stein ruled that the plaintiffs could not prove the government had orchestrated, approved, or acquiesced to the religious discrimination and the mere fact that the Salvation Army received money from the state was not enough to make it a "state actor" or its hiring practices attributable to the state. Indeed, Judge Stein concluded that the Salvation Army had a free exercise right to discriminate and "Nothing in the Constitution precludes . . . [the] Salvation Army's residual free exercise interest in selecting and managing its employees with reference to religion," even if those employees are technically paid by the state.

The other case, *Moeller v. Bradford County*, was settled out of court when Bradford County, Pennsylvania, corrections officials agreed not to fund religious activities or discriminatory hiring practices in prisoner rehabilitation programs. Americans United and the ACLU of Pennsylvania filed suit against the corrections officials and The Firm Foundation, a faith-based organization akin to Charles Colson's Prison Fellowship Ministries, in 2005 because federal, state, and local dollars funded a program which proselytized to inmates, pressured them to attend religious services, and hired only Christian employees. The Firm Foundation operated the Bradford County Correctional Facility's only vocational training program. The case was finally settled on June 5, 2007. The settlement required, among other things, that corrections officials and faith-based service providers obey regulations prohibiting public funds from "discriminating in hiring or employment based on religion."

It is quite possible that definitive rulings on religiously biased hiring practices for publicly funded secular jobs could take years or decades to arrive. The ethical calculus, I maintain, is squarely on the side of equality.

I'd like to think that overt religious discrimination is a thing of the past in American government. Unfortunately, it's not, and religious minorities suffer all too often from religious bigotry in our government, especially our military. People who practice religions that are particularly misunderstood by the majority are at the greatest risk for persecution. Wiccans come immediately to mind because they have been on the receiving end of a lot of discrimination lately. (Wicca is a nature-based faith with roots that predate Christianity. Many of its practitioners see divinity in nature and celebrate natural cycles like the phases of the moon and the seasonal equinoxes.)

Steven Goldsmith, President Bush's top aide responsible for implementing the faith-based initiative in its early years, was asked in 2001 if funding would be made available to minority religious groups, such as Wiccans. Apparently abandoning his boss's campaign promise "not [to] discriminate for or against Methodist or Mormons or Muslims or good people with no faith at all," Goldsmith

said he didn't "think that Wiccans would meet the standard of being humane providers of domestic violence shelters."

Goldsmith, it seems, was simply echoing a view long held both
outside and inside the administration. As governor of Texas, George
W. Bush opposed the Wiccans' right to meet at a military base in
that state. He actually went on ABC's *Good Morning America* shortly
before the 2000 presidential election and said he hoped officials at
Ft. Hood would rethink their decision to allow the meetings because
he didn't "think witchcraft [was] a religion." Sadly, it took the wars
in Iraq and Afghanistan to eliminate that prejudice in one of our
most far-reaching government entities: the Department of Veteran
Affairs (VA). Despite the First Amendment's prohibition on unduly
regulating religious exercise and expression, deceased Wiccan soldiers were not permitted to engrave their religious icon, the pentacle (a five-pointed star within a circle), on their memorial markers.

Thirty-eight other religious symbols were offered, ranging from
several versions of the Christian cross, to the Star of David, to the
Hindu Wheel of Righteousness to the atheist atom, but the VA
fought Roberta Stewart when she requested the pentacle for her
husband Patrick's memorial plaque. Patrick died when his Chinook
helicopter was shot down over Afghanistan in September 2005. For
over a decade the VA had stonewalled persistent Wiccans' requests
for appropriate grave markers (requests predating Roberta Stewart's), while the department approved symbols of a number of other
faiths, including an emblem for Sikhs, which was approved within
a matter of weeks.

Roberta Stewart contacted Americans United for help. AU tried
to negotiate with the VA, but we finally had to file suit in November 2006. Stewart and others, including Karen DePolito, whose husband, Korean War veteran Jerome Birnbaum, died in 2006; Circle
Sanctuary, a prominent Wiccan congregation; Jill Medicine Heart
Combs, whose husband, a military veteran, was severely ill; and
the Isis Invicta Military Mission, a Wiccan congregation serving military personnel were all named as plaintiffs in *Circle Sanctuary vs.
Nicholson*. It was disheartening to even have to deal with such overt
discrimination, but the case ended well. The VA finally came to its

senses in April 2007 and settled the case. Stewart and the other widows received their memorial markers in time for Memorial Day.

I love my work. Every day, I remind myself of how lucky—indeed, blessed—I am being able to earn my living defending the "first freedom." When I get to see the results reflected on a human level, there's no way to deny it. Rarely have I felt more joy than when I saw Roberta Stewart's face after our lawyers handed her the VA's new list of approved emblems of belief. The pentacle was at the bottom, emblem number 39.

Religious discrimination in our nation's military seems to haunt religious minorities in life, just as it does in death. The U.S. Air Force Academy in Colorado Springs, Colorado, was thrust into the spotlight in 2004 when football coach Fisher DeBerry hung a banner that read: "I am a Christian first and last. I am a member of Team Jesus Christ" in the team's locker room. Needless to say, not all Air Force cadets are Christians, nor do they play for "Team Jesus Christ;" they play for the U.S. Air Force Academy. The banner is just one more example of the military's insensitivity, at the very least, and hostility at the worst, toward religious diversity and church-state separation.

The problem of religious discrimination extends even to Congress. When Minnesota voters chose Keith Ellison as a member of the U.S. House of Representatives in November 2006, his election sparked a national controversy over the role of religion in political life. Ellison, a Muslim, announced shortly after his election that he would take his oath of office on the Qur'an when he was sworn in on January 4, 2007. As the first Muslim ever to serve in Congress, Ellison brought to light important questions—and misconceptions—about what the U.S. Constitution and American tradition require of public officials.

Within days of Ellison's election, right-wing Christian congressman Virgil Goode (R-VA) held him up as a reason why immigration reform was such an urgent need. Goode should have chosen someone else to demonize because Ellison isn't an immigrant; he can trace his family's presence in America back to 1742.

In a letter to his constituents, Goode wrote, "We need to stop illegal immigration totally and reduce legal immigration and end the diversity visas policy . . . allowing many persons from the Middle East to come to this country. I fear that in the next century we will have many more Muslims in the United States if we do not adopt the strict immigration policies that I believe are necessary to preserve the values and beliefs traditional to the United States of America."

Ironically, Goode represents the district that would be home to Thomas Jefferson if he were alive today. Ignoring the words of his most famous constituent, Goode railed against the representative-elect when he announced that he would take his oath of office on a Qur'an.

"The Muslim Representative from Minnesota was elected by the voters of that district and if American citizens don't wake up and adopt the Virgil Goode position on immigration, there will likely be many more Muslims elected to office and demanding the use of the Koran," Goode wrote to his constituents.

In an elegant symbolic gesture, Ellison was sworn in on a Qur'an that once belonged to Thomas Jefferson who, among other things, was a great student of religion. In fact Jefferson, in a letter to James Madison, exuded a sense of vindication when he wrote with satisfaction of the rejection of an amendment that lawmakers tried to add to a religious freedom bill he had drafted for passage by the Virginia legislature. The proposed amendment would have added a reference to Jesus Christ to the bill's preamble. By their rejection of the amendment, Jefferson wrote, the majority proved "that they meant to comprehend within the mantle of [the bill's] protection the Jew and Gentile, the Christian and the Mohametan, the Hindoo and the infidel of every denomination."

Sadly, the whole reaction was a spectacle, a chance for the Religious Right to claim that this is a "Christian Nation" and remind people of minority faiths that they are not welcome on its shores. It didn't even have to happen, because the Constitution is silent on oaths taken on religious texts. Article II, Section 1 of the U.S. Constitution requires the president-elect to take the following oath before assuming office: "I do solemnly swear (or affirm) that I will faithfully execute the Office of the President of the United States and will to the best of my ability, preserve, protect and defend the Constitution of the United States." Article VI requires that all other state and federal office holders "be bound by oath or affirmation to support this Constitution." (It goes on to say that "no religious test shall ever be required as a qualification to any office or public trust under the United States.") In fact, senators and representatives are sworn in *en masse* in their respective chambers. No religious text is even in the room for that exercise, but members often choose to pose for cameras with their hand on a religious text after the official swearing-in.

The examples in this section are merely illustrative. It is ironic that the Religious Right itself claims to be the victim of "anti-Christian" discrimination. When one compares the Religious Right's complaint that their government only put up a generic Christmas tree in the town square to Ms. Stewart's grievance that she could not put the symbol of her husband's faith on his gravestone, it's difficult to know whether to laugh or cry.

WORSHIP ... OR NOT

> *"You say you're supposed to be nice to the Episcopalians and the Presbyterians and the Methodists and this, that, and the other thing. Nonsense! I don't have to be nice to the spirit of the Antichrist."*
>
> PAT ROBERTSON, January 14, 1991, The 700 Club

No one can deny that the First Amendment protects religious liberty. That provision's guarantee of the "free exercise" of religion, while not absolute, provides a grand measure of religious liberty. Although most Americans identify with Christian denominations, the government is obligated to treat all religions equally. Christian sects do not receive preferential treatment simply because they are larger.

From a legal perspective, Christianity, Judaism, Islam, Buddhism, Hinduism, and all other two thousand religions in America stand on equal footing. But what about nonbelief—atheism, agnosticism, humanism, and so on? Is it protected by our Constitution?

Religious Right leaders are fond of saying that the Constitution protects freedom *of* religion but not freedom *from* religion. This is a simplistic and misguided rendering of a core freedom. The First Amendment would be of little value if it merely granted Americans the right to choose one religion among many. It must, and does, protect the right to reject them all.

The fact that it does so is cause for celebration because at the time of the Constitution's writing, it marked a major turning point in human rights. For many centuries, nonbelief was seen as a threat to public morals and an orderly society. Religious and governmental leaders believed that only religion—backed by its promise of eternal damnation for the wayward—could ensure proper behavior.

This belief was carried to the New World by the Europeans who settled on American shores. Many colonial charters and state constitutions limited public office to religious believers. Some went even further, insisting that public officials be "Trinitarian Protestants."

Not everyone agreed, and as the struggle for religious liberty began to play out, some advocates argued that what a person believed or did not believe about God should be irrelevant in his dealings with the state. It was, they argued, irrelevant to one's ability to lead people.

Colonial-era Baptist minister John Leland once observed, "If a man merits the confidence of his neighbors in Virginia—let him worship one God, twenty Gods or no God—be he Jew, Turk, Pagan, or Infidel, he is eligible to any office in the state."

Leland was not the only one to think this way. During debate over the Constitution, a South Carolina delegate named Charles Pinckney sponsored a measure stating that no religious qualification would ever be required for federal office.

The provision, found now in Article VI of the United States Constitution, states that those elected to public office may be "bound by Oath or Affirmation, to support this Constitution; but no religious

Test shall ever be required as a Qualification to any Office or public Trust under the United States."

This language is inconvenient for the Religious Right. Not only does it debunk claims that our country was founded to be a "Christian nation," it also makes it clear that atheists are duly qualified to hold federal office.

So atheists are free to run for the House of Representatives, the Senate, and the presidency. What about state and local governments?

Remarkably, the answer to those questions was not sorted out until 1961. Roy Torcaso, a Maryland man who served as a bookkeeper and office manager, was asked by his employer to become a notary public. Maryland had a constitutional provision limiting public office to those willing to make a "declaration of belief in the existence of God." Torcaso, an atheist, refused to make that statement.

Torcaso sued, and his case went all the way to the Supreme Court. In a unanimous ruling in Torcaso's favor, the Court declared in *Torcaso v. Watkins,* "We repeat and again reaffirm that neither a State nor the Federal Government can constitutionally force a person 'to profess a belief or disbelief in any religion.' Neither can constitutionally pass laws or impose requirements which aid all religions as against nonbelievers, and neither can aid those religions based on a belief in the existence of God as against those religions founded on different beliefs."

Maryland's provision, along with those in six other state constitutions, was made null and void. (Pennsylvania's is perhaps the most strangely worded. It holds that public office is open to anyone "who acknowledges the being of a God and a future state of rewards and punishments...." So to hold office in the Keystone State, you had to believe not only in God but also heaven and hell!)

Torcaso should have settled the matter, but in 1990, Herb Silverman, a professor of mathematics in South Carolina and an atheist, had to go to state court to challenge that state's bar on nonbelievers holding public office.

South Carolina's provision was very straightforward in its bigotry. It declared, "No person who denies the existence of a Supreme Being shall hold any office under this Constitution." Silverman applied to become a notary public to test the measure and won a unanimous ruling from the South Carolina Supreme Court.

These cases underline an important principle: the government is supposed to be neutral between belief and nonbelief. Obviously this is a difficult standard to reach sometimes. Governments often issue religious proclamations, acknowledging National Prayer Days and such. Religious symbols are posted at the seat of government, and the state does not hesitate to use religious phrases in a ceremonial fashion—"In God We Trust" on currency is one example.

Faith-based initiatives proliferate, and political leaders often talk about religion in glowing terms. Congress opens its sessions with prayer, as do state legislatures and many local governing bodies.

In what respect, then, is the state obligated to be neutral between belief and nonbelief? First, the government must protect a person's right not to be compelled to take part in religious worship. The government may not sponsor religious exercises in tax-funded institutions like public schools and require children to take part.

The government may not condition benefits on what a person believes or does not believe about religion. "Faith-based" initiatives are in my view dangerous in part because they threaten this principle. If tax money is turned over to a religious group to run a social service, that group might subtly or not so subtly pressure those in need to participate in religious activities as a condition of getting help.

Even making an inquiry about religion is taboo for the state. Census forms don't ask about religion for a good reason—it's none of the government's business where, if, when, or how you worship.

Atheists are protected in the secular workforce. Just as a person cannot be fired merely for being, say, a Roman Catholic or a Jew, a worker cannot be let go for declining to believe in God. Laws against religious discrimination encompass the religious skeptic.

In the public arena, organizations and individuals espousing nonbelief enjoy the same rights as religious groups. In some communities, religious groups have the right to use their own funds and resources to erect religious symbols on public property that is considered an "open forum." By law, this same right of access must be extended to all other groups.

If a Christian or Jewish group erects the Ten Commandments for a week in a town green in front of city hall, for example, that same right must be extended to a nonreligious group, which could post its secular moral principles or even a statement that "God Is Not Real."

Although the law on this matter is clear, it's undeniable that cultural biases against nonbelievers still exist in America. Article VI may ban religious tests for public office, but does that mean an open atheist can be elected? In fact, a near majority, 49 percent, tells pollsters they would not vote for an atheist for president—even if they liked his or her views. No other group has such high negatives.

Even as recently as the 2000 presidential election cycle, Democratic vice presidential candidate Joseph Lieberman suggested that religious believers are by default more moral than nonbelievers. After a barrage of criticism, led by Abraham Foxman of the Anti-Defamation League, the senator apologized for the remark.

To date, only one elected member of Congress, Representative Pete Stark (D-CA), has been willing to publicly announce that he does not hold a belief in a supreme being. Stark was joined by a state representative in Wisconsin and a few local officeholders in identifying themselves as nontheistic after the Secular Coalition for America announced it was trying to find an open nonbeliever who held public office.

Other forms of prejudice exist. Atheists are often publicly vilified and criticized in ways that would draw sharp rebukes if similar things were said about Jews or Muslims. Freedom of thought allows individuals to be bigots; it does not allow the government to promote bigotry.

The question of nonbelievers' rights has been controversial, and I think that is unfortunate. Although I am a Christian minister, I have no problem granting equal rights to those who reject all forms of religion. In fact, I insist that their rights be protected.

This should not be considered an unusual stand for a member of the clergy to adopt. In a sense, I am only following the best traditions of Leland, the Baptist minister I mentioned earlier. Leland knew that his rights as a Baptist were not secure unless the rights of everyone else were secure. He also knew that what a person believes about faith is not relevant to his or her ability to govern.

We all seek to be free from certain types of religion. In the nineteenth century, Roman Catholics objected to Protestant prayers and religious worship in public schools. The Catholic parents did not seek to infringe on the rights of their Protestant neighbors; they simply wanted their children to be free from an undue form of religious coercion. If a public school implemented daily prayers to an impersonal or "New Age"-type god, I expect many fundamentalist Christian parents would cry foul. These god concepts are not their own, so they do not want their children indoctrinated in them. They are seeking the same freedom from a specific religion that nonbelievers seek from all.

There is also a simple matter of justice and fairness involved. An honest advocate for religious freedom must contend for all faiths, even of those he or she may not personally approve. Roger Williams, the seventeenth-century religious liberty pioneer who founded Rhode Island, welcomed everyone into his colony. Williams sharply disagreed with the ruling Puritan establishment of Massachusetts, and he fled their reckless mixture of church and state. Williams welcomed other dissenters. For example, he was no fan of the doctrines of the Quakers, but allowed them to worship unmolested in Rhode Island during his watch.

We need to understand that in matters of conscience, we as a people are not truly free if some among us are oppressed. It is not enough to sit back and feel good about our own situation. Freedom of conscience is too valuable a gift not to be extended to all.

There are other reasons why "Worship . . . or Not" makes for good public policy. Among them is a simple question: what is the alternative? We have learned through bitter experience that coercion in matters of faith is counterproductive, cruel and downright un-American.

People cannot be compelled to believe certain things about religion. True, they can be terrorized into claiming that they believe certain things. They can be harassed and even imprisoned by repressive governments determined to stamp out "heresy." Their children can be indoctrinated in public institutions and turned against their own parents.

To what end? A belief or a nonbelief can be driven underground but never truly extinguished, except perhaps in a totalitarian state. A free society will not and cannot tolerate such things. Nor it is acceptable to imply that there is a certain set of shared values that make one truly "American," and that belief in God is one of these. Historically, Americans have been a churchgoing people, but our Constitution is secular and establishes no religious baselines for behavior.

I accept that there are certain shared civic values that tend to define the nation. Most Americans support democracy, free speech, the right to vote, and our system of government, for example. One can adopt these values without appending a religious creed to them.

Many people have, over the years, attempted to tie features of the American system of government to a religious perspective. I have heard Religious Right activists claim, for example, that a model for the U.S. government is found in the Bible.

I've read the Bible and have not been able to find it there. In fact, I find no examples of democracy in that book. It's not surprising, because the Bible was never intended to be a blueprint for government. This does not stop people from engaging in wishful thinking. The Bible, in my view, is a blueprint for faith and a guide for living a spiritual life. But not everyone chooses to live that life or to view the Bible in that manner. Some reject the fundamentalist gloss put on the Bible by certain believers, while others reject the book entirely.

Rather than bring the government into this spat, I'd just as soon leave it for the free marketplace of ideas. Debates and discussions about the nature of God, the existence of God, and the value of religion have been going on there in a robust fashion for a long time. Many voices seek to be heard, and the debate is often thought provoking. The government should allow all of these perspectives without endorsing any one.

Freedom of religion versus freedom from religion is a false dichotomy set up by the Religious Right to divide and confuse Americans. These two concepts do not fight one another. Indeed, they are closely related members of the same family of freedom. We best defend both at the same source: a high wall of separation between church and state.

RESPECT FOR ALL FAMILIES

> "We are moving against the tide in order to establish family and gender roles as described in God's word for the home and the family. If we do not do something to salvage the future of the home, both our denomination and our nation will be destroyed."
> PAIGE PATTERSON, Southwestern Baptist
> Theological Seminary President, 2007

What is a family? To hear the Religious Right tell it, you'd assume an American family is something straight out of the 1950s television show *Leave It to Beaver,* with one mother, one father (married only once and to each other), and their biological progeny living in a happy, churchgoing household. The Religious Right would also say that the ideal American family is under attack from a generation corrupted by licentiousness, women's liberation, Hollywood, and "anti-Christian" public education. This caricature, however, ignores historical and current reality because the American family has transformed itself over the years, yielding to a number of factors including economic trends, population patterns, and social ideology, to name a few.

Before the advent of single-family homes in suburbia, the basic unit of American society was more likely to be an extended family that occupied a house on a sprawling farm, or which populated several apartments on a city block. Life spans were considerably shorter than they are today, so a surviving spouse might have no economic choice but to remarry. Many nuclear families, just as they are today, were comprised of stepparents, half- and stepsiblings, or people considered to be relatives but not actually related by blood.

Women's social and economic liberation revolutionized relationships between men and women in the 1970s. Prior to this shift, it was very difficult for a married woman to get a divorce because most were economically dependent on their husbands. Even if she or her children were being abused, a woman could not flee a marriage if she could not support herself. Feminists pushed to loosen divorce laws in order to keep women from being trapped in dangerous situations and most states had adopted some form of "no-fault" divorce by the early 1980s. No-fault divorces are a way to annul a marriage without either spouse admitting wrongdoing, and they are one of the Religious Right's favorite targets. They see these compromises as nothing more than a way to avoid personal responsibility and "test-drive" married life.

The birth control pill (and the Supreme Court's rulings in *Griswold v. Connecticut* and *Eisenstadt v. Baird*) again revolutionized the American family because it made it possible to keep family sizes manageable in the industrialized, suburban landscape. Though still facing discrimination in education and work settings, women's ability to make choices about their own lives began to expand. As we discussed in "Reproductive Health," contraception and reproductive choice are key in the Religious Right's war on individual liberty.

Around the same time, gay people in urban centers such as New York and San Francisco began to publicly protest the discrimination and harassment they had suffered at the hands of police and other authorities. Both the women's movement and the gay rights movement found inspiration in the 1960s civil rights movements, which yielded federal legislation that ensured African Americans the right to vote, and protection from discrimination. The civil rights movement of the 1960s, women's rights movement of the 1970s, and gay rights movement of the 1980s ushered in a time of great societal change that gave the Religious Right the momentum it needed to build a powerful political base.

Fear and doubt often accompany change in societal norms. Fear and doubt are powerful tools, and the Religious Right has not wasted a moment exploiting those emotions to gain political power (the late Jerry Falwell, for example, famously blamed gay people and feminists for the terrorist attacks of September 11, 2001. At the time of Dr. Falwell's death Ann Coulter sent out an obituary column in which she said that the only thing she disagreed with Falwell about was that he didn't blame me and Senator Edward Kennedy for the attacks.)

The Religious Right is especially adept at this tactic when it comes to defending "traditional" marriage. The sacred institution, they say, is being destroyed and will implode the minute its civil privileges and responsibilities are accorded to gay men and lesbians. As the quote at the beginning of this chapter illustrates, some Religious Right leaders believe that their entire way of life is at stake.

Religious Right lawmakers tried an antidote to high divorce rates in the now defunct "covenant marriage." Beginning in 1997, couples in Louisiana, Arkansas, and Arizona could opt for a more restrictive form of civil marriage, which required premarital counseling and a witnessed declaration that the couple intends the marriage to be a lifelong commitment, and forbade divorce without evidence of abuse or adultery by one spouse, usually requiring a long waiting period before the divorce is finalized. To many, covenant marriages (a redundant term, since marriage is, by its nature, a covenant) represent a crude attempt to return to the era where a wife was her husband's property and could only escape a marriage if her life was in danger. Even then, a divorce was difficult to obtain, and destroyed rather than liberated a woman's life.

Researchers at Bowling Green State University who studied Louisiana's covenant marriages found that they had little impact on divorce rates. They did conclude, however, that people who opted for the covenant were fundamentally different from those who did not. The former group's rigid views of marriage and gender roles made them more likely to choose the covenant, while the latter's more liberal views made them opt for the status quo. Thus, couples who followed "traditional" family and gender roles were more likely to see divorce as a last resort; on the contrary, more liberal couples were likely to see divorce as a realistic option. It is interesting though, that divorce rates are generally higher in states where the Religious Right holds more sway than they are in more religiously diverse and politically liberal states. Massachusetts had the lowest in the nation in 2004, while Alabama, Arkansas, and Arizona had some of the highest rates in the nation. According to the 2000 U.S. Census, "the divorce rates in these conservative states are roughly 50 percent above the national average of 4.2 per thousand people."

Religious Right leaders are hardly willing to give up their fearmongering on the ostensible endangerment of the marriage institution by their political enemies. Public enemy number one, they say, is the gay and lesbian community. The push for marriage equality began in earnest in the mid-1990s, when three same-sex couples in Hawaii applied for marriage licenses. The applications tipped off a battle that led the governor to appoint an advisory committee in 1995. On December 8, 1995, a little more than a month before the 1996 Iowa caucus, Hawaii's Commission on Sexual Orientation and the Law recommended that the state, in the words of the *New York Times,* "grant marriage rights and responsibilities to couples of the same sex."

Religious Right leaders, many of whom were already unhappy with the Republican Party's front-running presidential contender, Senate majority leader Bob Dole, saw an opportunity to exploit the issue for political gain. A rally in "defense of marriage" was held at the First Federated Church of Des Moines the following February. All of the Republican candidates were expected to attend and sign a Marriage Protection Resolution, blown up to poster size, that codified opposition to gay marriage specifically, and gay rights in general. Nearly all the Caucus nominees—including Pat Buchanan —showed up that night to take in hand a large magic marker and put his or her name to the pledge. The rally's theme was a natural for Buchanan, who had made quite an impression four years earlier when he declared that the political parties were locked in a "cultural war . . . for the soul of America." On one side were the forces of cultural conservatism, and on the other side were "Clinton and Clinton" and the rest of the alleged liberal elite whose agenda, Buchanan said, comprised "abortion on demand, a litmus test for the Supreme Court, homosexual rights, discrimination against religious schools, [and] women in combat . . ." For what it is worth, on a recent edition of my daily radio show I asked Buchanan who is winning the "war" now, and without a pause, he said, "your side."

The 1996 Des Moines rally was doubtless a factor in Pat Buchanan's surprising strength in the Iowa caucus (Dole beat him by only a few points). Political pressure from conservative religious voters and lawmakers led to the Defense of Marriage Act (DOMA), passed and signed by President Bill Clinton later that year. The law says that no state may be made to recognize a same-sex marriage conducted under the auspices of another state. Many believe DOMA is unconstitutional, but given the current composition of the Supreme Court, it's unlikely that even the most carefully and accurately constructed constitutional arguments will trump the ideology of an increasing number of Supreme Court justices. While the thrust of the law is ostensibly to protect "states' rights," the law also bars same-sex couples from federal marriage rights and responsibilities. To name just one example, the law effectively deprives a gay man or lesbian of his or her partner's Social Security benefits.

Today, opposition to gay marriage remains a Religious Right battle cry, even though its leaders make a less-than-compelling case for its corrosive effect on heterosexual marriage. Most recently, the Supreme Judicial Court of Massachusetts' decision in 2004 to strike down as unconstitutional a law banning same-sex marriage has prompted new action by Congress. The Religious Right, led by President Bush, almost immediately stepped into the fray, calling for a "Federal Marriage Amendment" to the Constitution that would enshrine DOMA into our nation's founding document. If it were to pass Congress—it has failed a number of times, most recently in July 2006, when the House of Representatives rejected it 236 to 187 —and was ratified by the required two-thirds of the states, the Federal Marriage Amendment (FMA) would mark the first time that the Constitution was amended to discriminate against a particular class of people. In the past, we have added amendments to protect people from discrimination.

As if his call for a constitutional amendment banning same-sex marriage weren't enough, President Bush called upon the Congress to enforce a religious doctrine in its enactment. "Marriage cannot be severed from its cultural, religious, and natural roots without weakening the good influence of society," he said in a February 24, 2004, statement calling for the passage of the FMA. "Government, by recognizing and protecting marriage, serves the interests of all. Today I call upon the Congress to promptly pass, and to send to the states for ratification, an amendment to our Constitution defining and protecting marriage as a union of man and woman as husband and wife." Many other political leaders in the pro-FMA battle also demanded passage to preserve the "sanctity" of marriage—but then deny that this has any religious or "sacred" purpose. Senator Bill Frist, while also denying specific religious motivation, urged preservation of the "sacrament" of marriage.

Indeed, nothing in the ruling of the Massachusetts court would require any church or religious institution to confer marriage's religious privileges on same-sex couples. Despite access to no-fault divorce in all of the states, no judge has said that the Roman Catholic Church must honor divorce decrees issued by the state —and it does not. Divorces between Roman Catholics are not accepted by the church, as is the church's right under the Free Exercise Clause.

Marriage is a religious liberty issue because it is often a religious ceremony performed and recognized by the couple's church, but also carries with it great civil rights and responsibilities. Marriage, of course, can be an entirely secular event, but we walk down a dangerous path when we refuse to separate its religious and secular significance. As I discussed earlier, it is inevitable that religious doctrine will seep into the civil laws that govern every marriage. Government's refusal to recognize same-sex marriage is also a free exercise issue because it prohibits clergy from performing legal unions their religions view as legitimate. For example, clergy in the

United Church of Christ and the Unitarian Universalist Association and rabbis in the Reform Jewish traditions can and do perform same-sex marriages with the approval of the religious hierarchies of which they are a part. Nonetheless, state officials everywhere but Massachusetts will refuse to recognize these unions, while approving as many marriage certifications for heterosexual Baptists and Scientologists as come through the mail.

Even legislators who are nervous about agreeing to the religious liberty argument noted here often find it difficult to ignore the historical and ethical ramifications of artificially defining marriage. In 1967, the Supreme Court struck down Virginia's "Racial Integrity Act," which barred marriages between white and nonwhite people. "Marriage is one of the 'basic civil rights of man,' fundamental to our very existence and survival...." the Court held in *Loving v. Virginia*. It continued: "To deny this fundamental freedom on so unsupportable a basis as the racial classifications embodied in these statutes, classifications so directly subversive of the principle of equality at the heart of the Fourteenth Amendment, is surely to deprive all the State's citizens of liberty without due process of law." What reason is there to reject same-sex marriage if it is a fundamental right? Surely marriage's only purpose isn't to ensure our species' existence, since we don't require heterosexual couples to have children. We don't force them to do much more than pay taxes (often at lower rate than taxpayers of the "single" persuasion).

Since the Federal Marriage Amendment did not pass, Religious Right activists continue to press for amendments to state constitutions to define marriage in the same way as the FMA would. Some would go even further, opting to bar any form of relationship that grants any benefits to unmarried persons (straight or gay) comparable to those in the *Leave It to Beaver* households in the state.

An elegant solution exists to the controversy of gay marriage but, unfortunately, it's one that its enemies often find hard to accept, since it would buttress the separation of church and state. I alluded to the solution earlier. Since marriage is a religious institution, get government out of the marriage business. The government can offer civil unions for any two consenting adults who request them, and it will be the government's job to enforce the property, contract, and custody laws implied.

Let "marriage," then, as a religious institution, be given its shape and sacred role by the faith tradition in which one marries. (In Europe, a part of the religious ceremony in some cities often includes an interlude, sometimes by carriage, in which the couple go to the town clerk's office and sign the papers for their marriage before completing the religious event.) In the event of divorce, the government shall enforce the law with regard to the civil union, leaving it to the faith tradition to decide whether or not to withhold sacraments from the disunited couple or take any other kind of adverse actions.

Separating civil unions and marriage would also absolve us of the propensity to use religious law to settle child custody disputes. Sadly, the Religious Right seems to have little difficulty letting courts use biblical standards to decide how a child is raised. For example, in 2002, Alabama Supreme Court chief justice Roy Moore (the jurist who was famously removed from the bench after refusing to take down a mammoth Ten Commandments sculpture that the federal courts had found unconstitutional) issued a separate thirty-page opinion in which he joined his colleagues in denying the right of a lesbian mother to gain custody of her daughter.

Moore's diatribe took a more "expansive" view of the issue, calling homosexuality "detestable and abominable" and an "inherent evil" that goes against biblical scripture and Alabama law. The state, he said, had an interest in preserving the "fundamental family structure" and "carries the power of the sword, that is, the power to prohibit conduct with physical penalties, such as confinement and even execution. It must use that power to prevent the subversion of children toward this lifestyle, to not encourage a criminal lifestyle." It seems the chief justice believed it was legally and morally acceptable to incarcerate and execute alleged human "threats" to the "fundamental family structure."

One particularly creative Religious Right "thinker" has combined what he sees as the evils of divorce law with the evils of ho-mosexuality and state intervention on behalf of children abused by their families to create an all-encompassing conspiracy theory. The thinker is Stephen Baskerville, who is peddling a doomsday sce-nario in which the state comes in, takes your children under a false accusation of child abuse, gives them to gay parents for adoption, and kicks you out of your house just because your wife doesn't want to be married to you anymore. Here's an excerpt from a 2004 Baskerville column titled, "Could your kids be given to 'gay' parents?"

> Child abuse is overwhelmingly a phenomenon of single-parent homes. Government and feminist propaganda suggest that single-parent homes result from paternal abandonment. In fact, they are usually created by family court judges, who have close ties to the social service agencies that need children. By forcibly removing fathers from the home through unilateral or "no-fault" divorce, family courts create the environment most conducive to child abuse and initiate the process that leads to removal of the children from the mother, foster care, and adop-tion. Gay adoption is simply the logical culmination in the process of turning children into political instruments for gov-ernment officials.

American society has actually made great strides in recognizing the rights of gay parents. In only three states is there a complete ban on gay adoption: Florida, Mississippi, and Utah. As I write this, legislative efforts are under way in Florida to lift the ban.

Ours is a nation whose people are diverse in many ways—not just ethnically and religiously, but even culturally. American fami-lies have long taken different shapes and, in fact, appear to be re-forming as extended families, forced by the economic pressures of real estate and health care costs. Many permutations are possible in the future. Children need to be protected from true threats to their well-being, but lack of accessible health care will do them more harm than would adoption by gay couples who very badly wish to raise children. Women need the freedom to leave destructive marriages. No, divorce is hardly a desirable result, but a woman trapped in a desperate situation does not enhance our society. Allow the Religious Right to have its way with family law, and there will be no end to the state's meddling in our family lives.

Resources: A Call to Action

MIKE KEEFE, DENVER POST

Frequently Asked Questions
Related to Our First Freedom

1. What is religious freedom?

Religious freedom means that every person is free to make a decision about religion—to affirm, embrace, and practice religion privately and publicly or to reject it as a matter of conscience and conviction. Within the framework of the United States Government, religious freedom is synonymous with constitutional guarantees that the government will never establish an official religion amid other religions, or establish religion over nonreligion, *and* that every person is free to express his or her religion publicly, so long as that expression does not compromise another person's freedom.

2. Why do people call religious freedom America's "first freedom?"

Religious freedom is called our first freedom because it was the first freedom guaranteed by the United States Constitution and the freedom that formed the foundation on which other freedoms were constructed.

3. What does church-state separation have to do with religious freedom?

The wall of separation between church and state is the institutional application of the religious freedom guaranteed to every citizen of our nation. Though the specific words, "a wall of separation between church and state," do not appear in the Constitution, this famous metaphor, popularized by Jefferson, captures the meaning and application of religious freedom as guaranteed in the Constitution. The founders of the nation knew firsthand that entanglement between the institutions of religion and government spelled trouble for both religion and government.

4. Why is it important?

At stake in the fate of religious freedom is nothing less than the success or failure of democracy as envisioned and described in the United States Constitution and experienced by all citizens. In other words, the future of America's first freedom will determine to a great extent the future of the form of government and the way of life at the center of the vision that motivated and informed the founders of this nation. Should the moment ever arrive when Americans completely turn their attention away from the importance of religious liberty and cease to protect it vigorously, that will be the moment the fate of democracy hangs dangerously in the balance.

5. Does the First Amendment guarantee only freedom *for* religion or does it also guarantee freedom *from* religion?

Framers of the Constitution understood the importance of freedom and never would have allowed a provision called freedom that made no provision for choices. The Constitution provides for people to choose for or against religion. President Franklin Roosevelt spoke to this issue with great clarity: "The traditional Jeffersonian principle of religious freedom was so broadly democratic that it included the right to have no religion at all—it gave to the individual the right to worship any God he chose or no god."

6. Does separation of church and state mean that religious beliefs and values should have no role in or influence on politics or government?

Institutional separation between religion and government is not synonymous with divorcing religion and government in personal citizenship. Individuals invariably bring to their involvement in government beliefs and values born and nurtured by their religions or their nonreligious ideologies. But any entanglement between religious institutions and government institutions is bad news for the Constitution, a problem for religion, and a serious threat to government by democracy.

7. Isn't America a Christian nation?

More Christians live in the United States right now than have ever lived in any other land in the history of the world. But large numbers of people identified with Christianity does not make the nation "Christian." Supporters of the "Christian nation" theory about the United States cherry-pick quotations from various founders of the nation to defend their claim. Not only is the claim that America is a Christian nation historically inaccurate, it is also, from one Christian perspective, a theological heresy.

8. Weren't our Founding Fathers deeply religious men?

Most of the founders were far from the kind of avid believers in the Lordship of Jesus Christ and devotion to the Trinitarian God generally associated with Christianity. In fact, at the time of the Revolution, only 10 to 15 percent of the people belonged to any church.

9. How come conservatives and liberals seem to define religious liberty in two completely different ways?

Religious freedom has a specific meaning, not to be confused with rhetoric of religious freedom that affirms freedom *for* but not *from* religion, or with a strategy for destroying the historic wall of separation between church and state.

10. What's wrong with a church being reimbursed by the government for providing social services to those in need?

When religious entities become dependent upon government money, seldom do their leaders have the courage to challenge the government's wrongdoing. It seems better to get money for a ministry than to risk the loss of that money by raising questions or making charges related to the morality of business and government no-bid contracts, preemptive military strikes against another nation, the torture of prisoners, or the burgeoning domestic problems in the areas of education, health care, and energy. Religious leaders who accept government subsidies to fund their ministries, thus becoming contract employees of federal agencies, seldom want to be prophetic and risk their employer being offended enough to cut off funding.

11. Aren't people who are pro-church-state separation anti-religion?

The most intense advocates for the secular nature of the United States government have been the people most respectful of religion and devoted to preserving the integrity of religion.

12. What does this have to do with *me?*

Religious freedom will continue as a friend to religious and non-religious citizens alike and as a pivotal contributor to the strength of our democracy, as long as citizens of this nation have the will that it continue and express that will through public advocacy and political action. Only as people recognize the inseparable connection between popular social-political issues—government-funded religious activities, legislative attempts to impose sectarian values on the nation by means of government agencies, forced recitations of Christian prayers in public school classrooms, and government support for private religious schools, to cite only a few examples—and the impact of those issues on the constitutional provision of religious freedom, will they be motivated to pick up that cause with the same intense enthusiasm they give to other causes.

Twenty Reasons Why You Need to Protect Religious Liberty and Separation of the Institutions of Religion and Government

1. Religious freedom guarantees every person the right to freely practice religion or to abstain from religion. In order for society to benefit, religious belief and practice *must* be free and voluntary.

2. Both history and current events show us that increasingly, religion (in particular one narrow religious view) is being used as a tool to influence policy and advance political strategy. America's shared values are being replaced by values that advance only particular sectarian interests. Policymakers and elected officials should not give preferential treatment to one particular religious voice. We Americans must remain able to choose to freely live our lives.

3. In matters of faith, government must not take sides. Religious freedom assures all citizens that the nation will not establish one religion over another or even favor religion over nonreligion. When the institutions of religion and government are kept separate, what you believe or don't believe about religion has no relevance to your standing with the government. You cannot be defined as a second-class citizen.

4. You should never be forced to live under someone else's religion. Of course, politics should be moral, but unions of religion and government tend to bring about either tyranny or a devitalized state-established church.

5. A secular government is best for all people—a government profoundly appreciative of religion but totally disinterested in being controlled by religion or in controlling religion.

6. Your parental rights should be protected, and your children should never be coerced to take part in religious exercises in public schools. When religion and government are kept separate, you have the right to direct what, if any, religious upbringing your children receive. No public school official or other agent of the government will make that decision for you.

7. Separating religion and government ensures that members of the clergy—not government officials—guide your religious life, and the religious lives of all Americans. A proper division of religion and government means that lawmakers focus on legislating, while religious leaders focus on spiritual matters.

8. Religious liberty is absolutely crucial to protecting religious pluralism as a prized trait of our nation. America is home to thousands of religious denominations and nonreligious philosophies. Because the government officially sanctions none, all are free to flourish. Separating religion and government leads to great vitality and diversity among religious groups, and provides a basis for interreligious cooperation. And real solutions for the problems addressing our nation can only come when people who represent and appreciate this diversity are included in the public dialogue.

9. Disentangling the institutions of religion and government protects the integrity of science by keeping religiously grounded concepts like creationism and intelligent design out of the public school classroom. Separation ensures that religion does not usurp the role of science in public institutions. It recognizes that science and religion generally ask different questions and employ different methodologies to answer these questions.

10. Disentangling the institutions of religion and government promotes a spirit of free inquiry in medicine and science. If narrow religious perspectives control science and medicine, some promising forms of medical research and scientific advances will be retarded. Science forced to bow to religious ideology can never achieve its true potential.

11. When religion and government are kept apart, you cannot be forced to pay for someone else's religion. You are free, under church-state separation, to subsidize only the faith of your choice (or refuse to subsidize any). Mandatory taxation for religion, which is common in countries that do not have separation of religion and government, violates this fundamental right.

12. When religion and government are independent of each other, the job of displaying and maintaining religious symbols is in the hands of religious groups, not government. Government endorsement of certain religious symbols implies that all citizens support those symbols.

13. By separating religion and government, we make sure that our laws are based on neutral and secular principles, not religious ideology. The American Constitution is a secular document, and our laws are not based on any type of theology or religious perspective.

14. Individual freedoms are more likely to be protected when religion and government are kept separate. For instance, under the separation principle, religious groups cannot impose scripturally interpreted views of sexuality on everyone through the legislative process. Nor can they deny gay people their rights, simply because homosexuality offends some religious believers.

15. Women's rights are more likely to be protected when religion and government are kept separate. The rights of women are often sharply curtailed in nations that merge religion and government. In some theocratic nations, women cannot vote, drive, or go outside unaccompanied by a male relative.

16. Separating religion and government protects the vitality of houses of worship by making them solely responsible for their financial upkeep. Houses of worship must stand or fall on their own, based on voluntary contributions. They cannot rely on the government for handouts. This voluntary principle makes our houses of worship vital and strong, and prevents them from becoming political pawns.

17. When religion and government are independent, religious leaders are not expected to become advocates for particular candidates or political parties, nor do they expect to be punished or rewarded because of their positions on partisan political issues. Religious institutions must not be held accountable to the priorities and interests of federal, state, or local governments.

18. Censorship based on religious sensibilities is less likely when religion and government are kept separate. Thanks to separation of church and state, religious groups cannot censor books, plays, music, or art simply because they may offend the sensibilities of some believers.

19. When religion and government are kept separate, all religious groups that are willing to abide by secular laws enjoy the same rights and freedoms. A group cannot be persecuted or shut down just because its doctrines are unpopular or misunderstood. Its members cannot be harassed or treated with disdain by the government based on their beliefs.

20. No citizen's rights or opportunities should depend on religious beliefs or practices. Church-state separation guarantees that if government forms a partnership with religious groups (for example, in aiding victims of a natural disaster), tax funds will not be used to promote religion and will be made available only to religious groups that hire workers on the basis of qualifications, not religious beliefs. People will be able to get help from government without having to sacrifice their civil and religious freedoms.

Ten Things You Can Do to Protect Religious Liberty in Your Community, State, and Nation

1. Join groups like The Interfaith Alliance and Americans United for Separation of Church and State. These national organizations fight every day to protect your freedom to worship, or not, as you choose. Support them financially and join local chapters, if they exist in your area. Consider starting a local, grassroots group.

2. Register and vote. Take part in local, state, and national elections. Educate yourself about where candidates stand on important issues. Attend candidate forums. Question candidates, especially local school board contenders, on where they stand on issues at the intersection of religion and politics. Remember to be specific. Ask, for example, whether they support the teaching of intelligent design or back comprehensive sex education programs.

3. Urge your local media to interview the candidates as well. Especially when candidates persist in talking about their religion on the campaign trail, you have a right to receive answers to questions such as: How will you show respect for the religious pluralism in this nation? Do you support the religious freedom clauses in the Constitution? Do you support the institutional separation of religion and government? How will your religion impact your decisions on public policy?

4. Be heard. Start simply, by speaking with your friends and neighbors and letting them know why religious freedom is important to you. Then write letters to the editor about issues at the intersection of religion and politics. Respond to writers and columnists who advance theocratic views. Don't be afraid to call in to talk radio shows, especially ones with ultraconservative hosts. Make cogent, polite, and informed comments to rebut their arguments.

5. Encourage interfaith cooperation. Religious pluralism is vital in a society marked by so many different religions and philosophies. Visit a house of worship different from your faith tradition. Support efforts that increase understanding and respect among faiths and that encourage religious leaders to work together.

6. Attend your member of Congress's town hall meeting and ask her or him The Interfaith Alliance's Five Questions to learn about her or his positions on religious liberty and pluralism (see the section entitled Election-year opportunities in the chapter Strengthening Democracy: Confronting Challenges and Seizing Opportunities, page 000).

7. Educate the next generation. Help young people understand the importance of defending religious liberty and the separation of church and state. If our freedoms are to survive, they must have the active support of a new generation of leaders. Urge students to form clubs in their schools to discuss these constitutional issues.

8. Support public education and libraries. Opponents of the separation of religion and government seek to undermine our public schools and libraries or infuse them with sectarian dogma. Help keep these vital, taxpayer-supported institutions open and welcoming to students of all religious and philosophical backgrounds.

9. Take advantage of new media. Blogs, MySpace pages, Internet-based social networking, and other forms of new media are great ways to reach lots of people for very little expense and time. Use any forum you can to talk about why religious freedom is important to you.

10. Take material about religious liberty issues or copies of The Interfaith Alliance or Americans United for Separation of Church and State publications to bookstores, coffeehouses, houses of worship, and other gathering places, and ask if you can put them out for free distribution.

MIKE KEEFE, *DENVER POST*

Acknowledgments

The publication of this book, like participation in the entire First Freedom First campaign, has been a venture in expansive cooperation.

Seldom does it happen, but in bringing together this publication, every single person to whom I turned for help said "yes" immediately. First among those was Barry Lynn, who consented on the spot to work with me on the content of the book. No sooner had I proposed the idea of the book to Helene Atwan, director of Beacon Press, than she said, "We are the ones to do this book, and we want to do it." Tom Hallock encouraged the process and offered an amazing degree of flexibility in dealing with a traditionally inflexible publication schedule. Our editor, Brian Halley, has been a model of patience as well as a tremendous source of helpful counsel and other forms of support, personally and professionally.

Board members and staff members of the Grove Foundation have expressed an unusually high degree of interest in and made multiple suggestions regarding this whole campaign generally and this publication specifically. Special thanks go to Eva Grove, Karen Grove, and Rebekah Saul Butler. Andy Grove has been tenacious in his devotion to the First Freedom First campaign and gracious in his willingness to contribute a moving personal perspective on religious freedom to this volume.

I am grateful for the level of interest in and dedication to this project demonstrated by members of the staff of The Interfaith Alliance Foundation. Barry, I know, extends special thanks to writer/researcher Adele Stan and to Americans United's Rob Boston and Lauren Smith for lending enormous time and talent researching and editing his contributions to the book. Both of us acknowledge with gratitude Donna Redwing and Eric Schutt from The Interfaith Alliance Foundation and Beth Corbin and Bethany Moore from Americans United for Separation of Church and State for the day-to-day guidance they have given to the educational efforts of the First Freedom First initiative.

Thaler Pekar, principal of Thaler Pekar & Partners, who serves as a communications consultant with The Interfaith Alliance Foundation, has devoted untold hours to reading and rereading the entire manuscript so as to assure that the important message in this volume is communicated well. Thaler's assistance has been as constantly available as it has been tangibly invaluable.

Finally, but very importantly, Mike Keefe provided a serendipitous gift to all of us when he agreed to allow us to print several of his cartoons in the book. Keefe is the award-winning cartoonist for the *Denver Post* whose sensitive, skilled sketches speak louder than words, simplifying the complex and aiding understanding of a wide variety of issues related to religious freedom.

Cooperation has its challenges. But a shared belief in the importance of protecting the precious treasure of religious freedom and its corollary of church-state separation has sustained all involved in this project through the challenges and brought us to this moment of gratitude for the people and the work that have made this book possible.

C. WELTON GADDY